Soul RESCUE

How to Break Free from Narcissistic Abuse & Heal Trauma

DANA ARCURI, CTRC

Soul Rescue: How to Break Free from Narcissistic Abuse & Heal Trauma

Printed in the United States of America

ISBN: 978-0-9910768-9-5

Book cover and formatting by Trisha Fuentes

Dedication

I dedicate my book, *Soul Rescue*, to my three adult children; Tony, Jenna, and Ryanna. In my younger days, I was not aware of or educated about narcissistic abuse, narcissistic personality disorder, and intergenerational trauma, nor had I understood my own past abuse history.

Soul Rescue is the book that I wish I could have read before I became a mother. Had I known 30 years ago what I know now, I guarantee that I would have raised each of my children much differently. I would have taken greater measures to protect each of my kids from the offenders within our birth family.

Tony, Jenna, and Ryanna have taught me about authentic love, boundaries, and trusting my gut instincts. All three of them have given me the courage to stand up for myself and to end the cycle of abuse within my family of origin.

May each of my beautiful children know they are worthy of caring, healthy, respectful relationships. May you be the positive change for the next generation. Thank you for your continued love, wisdom, and emotional support.

All of My Love,
Mom XOXO

Medical Disclaimer

This book is not intended as a substitute for the medical advice of physicians, psychiatrists, or therapists. It shall not take the place of a medical or psychiatric evaluation, diagnosis, and/or treatment. The contents inside this book are for educational purposes, advocacy, and to build awareness. It is based on my personal experience, education, knowledge, and facts gathered during extensive research. The information inside this book does not constitute medical or mental health advice. The accuracy of the information is not guaranteed. Furthermore, individuals are recommended to seek professional medical attention in the event they are suffering mental health concerns and/or medical conditions.

Trigger Warning

Some of the chapters in this self-help book may contain information with minor graphic content. If you have experienced child abuse, mental abuse, narcissistic abuse, physical abuse, spiritual abuse, sexual assault, domestic violence, Complex PTSD/PTSD, or trauma, the content may trigger a response.

Please be aware that triggers are a common and normal part of the trauma recovery process. Triggers are a clear sign that there is more recovery needed. The triggers are an opportunity to go deeper into your traumatic event, to process it, acknowledge it, and to promote helpful strategies for your healing journey. Please use discretion and read with care.

Author Notes

As the author of *Soul Rescue: How to Break Free from Narcissistic Abuse & Heal Trauma,* I have written my recollection of real-life events to the best of my knowledge. The content within these pages were based on my educational, personal, and professional experiences. Furthermore, the book content contains information based on my perceptions, understanding, and my conscious reality of my traumatic experiences.

The names of some people, places, and identifying details have been changed in order to protect their privacy. It is my sincere wish that *Soul Rescue* will be a positive source of credible education, information, inspiration, support, advocacy, healing, and hope. Most importantly, may this self-help book provide you with helpful tools to build awareness about the insidious aftermath of trauma and all forms of abuse, including narcissistic abuse.

Contents

ONE

Dazed & Confused

"Many victims of narcissistic abuse continue in their relationship hoping that things will get better and when they don't, they are left confused, dazed and emotionally wrecked. It is important to see the signs of narcissistic abuse in order to not fall victim to its trap as you are made to believe that it is all in your head."

Lynda Cameron Price, Licensed Counselor

Two words sum up being the daughter of a narcissistic mother: deep sorrow. It was like a massive boulder sat on my chest. Choking me. Suffocating me. Drowning me. Spinning my life out of control. My memories of growing up to become an adult woman who suffered ritual narcissistic abuse had a common thread: Tears. Drama. And compounded trauma.

Underneath it was a thick layer of toxic shame and utter horror. The horror of living through unspeakable things. Divorced parents who were emotionally absent. Child neglect and abuse that carried throughout my adult years. A dysfunctional family. Abusive siblings.

Brutal betrayal by my blood relatives. Unhealthy patterns, which left me dazed and confused.

I am the youngest daughter of five girls. I was groomed early on to become a people-pleaser. A peacemaker. To be compliant. Even if it meant staying silent. To overlook the misdeeds of others. To not talk about my dark family secrets.

As a child, my silence is what saved me. It became my adaptive coping mechanism. It helped me to survive abuse. To avoid the truth. To stuff my pain. To minimize my turmoil. To pretend that everything was fine. Little Dana learned to be a big girl and to not cry.

For five long, grueling decades, I've lived beneath a fog. The heavy cloak blinded me. It smothered me. For years, I felt completely unaware of the unhealthy state of my birth family. I didn't understand it or acknowledge it. Clouded by chaos, I had been incoherent of my own conscious reality.

False Guilt & Living in Denial

The truth about narcissistic abuse is that it hurts. Yes, it hurts badly. The burden feels too heavy. Unconsciously, in our early stages of narcissistic abuse we may deny our reality. There's a part of us who has difficulty wrapping our brain around our loved one who intentionally harmed us.

We cannot face the fact that this person who we love is repeatedly inflicting pain onto us. That they're purposely hurting us. Habitually, the narcissist dumps their guilt and toxic shame onto us. This person can be our mother, father, sibling, relative, spouse, or intimate partner.

They bounce between loving and cruel behaviors. One minute they are super sweet to us. The next minute, they fly into an uncontrollable rage. They freak out, flip out, and lash out at us. It can be verbal abuse, physical abuse, or both.

In my experience with my narcissistic mother, I never knew what to expect. On a daily basis, I walked on eggshells around her. From one moment to the next, I learned to expect the unexpected. At the slightest dispute, my mom criticized me, screamed at me, and blame-shifted me.

Following our disagreement, she'd ignore me, stonewall me, and find sly ways to punish me. Sometimes she would go weeks without calling me. She'd gossip about me to my four sisters. She'd go out to dinner with them and exclude me. She'd play the 'victim card,' claiming that I verbally attacked her. Yet, in reality she was the guilty one of psychologically harming me. Not just once or twice. Rather, it was over and over in a painful cycle of abuse.

Through the years, I had such a difficult time grappling with this. How do we come to terms with narcissistic abuse? How do we accept that our mother (or sibling, spouse, partner, etc.) has malicious intentions to hurt us? How do we deal with a narcissist who groomed us to become helpless? How do we come to terms after they've stripped us of our dignity?

Oftentimes, the scapegoat feels worthless and powerless. After being beaten down, year after year, we have a strong sense of false guilt. Unconsciously, we take the narcissist's guilt as if it were our own. As if it were our fault. As if we are deserving of mental torture and physical abuse.

We abandon ourselves. We stay loyal and loving to the narcissist. We spend years consumed in denial and suppressed memories. We carry a heavy load of guilt, which isn't even ours.

False guilt is feeling guilty when one is not actually guilty. Genuine guilt is a result of wrongdoing. It is appropriate to feel guilty if we had done something wrong. However, false guilt is rooted in deception, denial, and dysfunction. It is directly connected to our destructive and codependent relationship with a narcissist.

False guilt teaches us four lies:

1. You are bad
2. It's your fault
3. You should be ashamed of yourself
4. You are powerless

As I type this chapter, my inner child weeps. She grieves the mother she never had. The lost years. The toxic family betrayal. She laments her stolen childhood. She aches for everything the narcissist took from her. My inner child deeply mourns her agonizing years of living in denial. She's heartbroken for carrying false guilt and for being bullied into silence.

Trauma Wounds Run Deep

Narcissistic abuse is cited as being 'soul murder.' It not only breaks your heart and crushes your spirit, but it's directly linked to trauma wounds. Trauma pierces your core essence. It breaks you into dozens of pieces. Your trauma runs deep. Unaware, you may carry it into your adulthood.

If we ignore our abuse and trauma, it will continue to reveal itself to us. It may be subtle or it may be intense. Trauma can show up in our sleep. We may battle insomnia and nightmares. We can experience physical pain and emotional distress. We may struggle with anxiety and depression. Or we may suffer hypervigilance, dissociation, and Complex PTSD/PTSD.

We may have flashbacks. We may battle triggers. Or we can suddenly be slammed with fight, flight, freeze, or fawn mode. Each of these signs are a normal trauma response. Even if we are unaware that it's linked to our emotional trauma.

When our fragmented memories surface, initially we may look the other way. We may not face it. We dare not open up that can of worms. Why? Because trauma haunts us. It is within our body and our subconscious minds. Our trauma creates a bloody, gaping wound that's excruciating. Our natural instinct is to run away.

We may not know how to fix it or change it. We may not know where to start. Interpersonal trauma is not something we can simply forget, nor get over. Even if we wanted to let go of our past trauma, our body won't forget. Trauma is enmeshed in our brain and cells; epigenetics and cellular memory. Our body keeps the score.

After being battered, bruised, and betrayed, we typically won't disclose it. Not to anyone. Not as a child and not as an adult. During our early stages of narcissistic abuse, we may feel humiliated, ashamed, and devastated.

Wrestling for our sanity, we cannot make logical sense out of the narcissist's devious schemes. We are mystified by their nonstop gaslighting, manipulation, and covert tactics. Their hostile words, actions, and behaviors behind closed doors have become the norm.

By now, we've become accustomed to a three-ring circus by our narcissistic parent, relative, spouse, or partner. What is abnormal in our society has been twisted into normal to the scapegoat. We've become accustomed to bullying, retaliation, and smear campaigns against us.

Child Neglect & Abuse

Child neglect and abuse is a hidden epidemic. The topic is taboo. Surviving abusive relationships, especially in the family unit, is complicated. Oftentimes, victims of child abuse, sexual assaults, domestic violence, and narcissistic abuse don't report it.

During my extensive research, I discovered that most children don't disclose their sexual abuse, until late in life. On the website, Child USA, they share about delayed disclosure. *"Most child victims of sexual assault disclose, if they disclose at all, during adulthood, with a median age of 48 and an average age of 52."*

When I was three-years old and my babysitter abused me, I didn't have the vocabulary, maturity, nor the ability to disclose it. As a little girl, I felt helpless and powerless. For two terrible years, the teen caregiver stole my innocence. She was a malicious monster! She robbed me of my childhood. She nearly scarred me for life.

Trauma wounds are invisible. We cannot see visible bruises, cuts, or scars. Yet, if we don't tend to them, we can carry them throughout our lives. We may relive our trauma over and over.

Common Reasons Why Children Don't Disclose Abuse:

- **Keep it a Secret** - Predators and abusers are masters of manipulation. They will instruct or enforce children to keep it a secret.
- **Threats:** Another common tactic used by perpetrators is to threaten a child and instill fear in them to be quiet. Abusers intimidate children to not tell anyone about the abuse and/or sexual assaults.
- **Lack of Maturity** - Similar to my situation, children cannot find the words to describe what someone has done to them; physically, mentally, and sexually. Due to their immaturity and inexperience, they don't know the correct terms for body parts, nor do they understand inappropriate touch.
- **Victim-blaming & Toxic-shaming** - Predators will blame the child for the abuse. They accuse the child of causing it to happen, which is rooted to toxic-shame. The child is told that it's their fault, which leads to the child feeling ashamed and like a 'bad person.'
- **Grooming** - Early on, the abuser will find covert ways to earn the child's trust and compliance. In many cases, predators earn the trust of the child's parents, too. Grooming enables the predator to continue inappropriate touch. It usually escalates into sexual advances.

- **No One Will Believe You** - The offenders discredit the child, claiming that everything is a figment of their imagination. They use clever ways to silence the child. They insist, *"No one will believe you!"*
- **Punishment** - Perpetrators can physically, mentally, and/or sexually harm the child in order to silence them. The abusers may threaten them. They may say that if their parents learn the truth, their mom and dad will punish them, too.
- **Dissociation** - This is defined as disruptions in aspects of consciousness, identity, memory, physical actions and/or the environment. The causes of dissociation usually include trauma, often prolonged trauma, such as physical, mental, or sexual abuse, in childhood. Sometimes, children who dissociate from traumatic events don't remember the abuse, until later in the future.
- **Love & Loyalty** - According to ArkOfHopeForChildren.org, *"90% of children knew their abuser."* Despite the abuse, children may trust and love the person who hurts them. They can remain loyal to the abuser. For example, a child wants to protect their mom, dad, grandpa, or sibling if that person's abusing him or her; physically, mentally, sexually, and/or spiritually. No doubt, the child is dazed and confused.

In my early childhood through adulthood, I lived in survival mode. For me, it meant to not speak about my past neglect and abuse. To bury my frightful memories. To try to forget the despicable things that happened to me.

No matter how hard I tried to suppress my trauma, it continued to plague me. Out of nowhere, I'd be triggered. Boom! A gruesome reminder of my abuse would show up. A dozen negative emotions and sensations swept through me. Fear, sadness, anger, confusion, powerlessness, numb, tense, and drained.

These triggers happened in my sleep and my waking state. All of my five senses were on high alert. Sometimes, triggers occurred when I heard a song from the 1970's, which transported me back to my childhood. Instantly, terrifying memories caught me off guard. My body automatically experienced fight, flight, freeze, or fawn.

Fawn is the fourth trauma response. I've noticed that it's rarely discussed on social media when talking about abuse. Fawn is best understood as people-pleasing. Fawn is linked to our loyalty, especially to the narcissistic parent. Isn't it just like naive kids to try to please their parents or other adults? To be cooperative and compliant?

As a child, that was me. Little Dana was a good girl. She obeyed those in authority. She submitted to them. She did as she was told to do. She didn't want to ruffle anyone's feathers. She desperately wanted to win the approval, love, and acceptance of others, including her mom. She wanted to make everyone happy.

Pete Walker, M.A., MFT, has coined the term 'fawn' as it relates to trauma, explains, "*Fawn types seek safety by merging with the wishes, needs and demands of others. They act as if they unconsciously believe that the price of admission to any relationship is the forfeiture of all their needs, rights, preferences and boundaries. They often begin life like the precocious children described in Alice Miler's 'The Drama Of The Gifted Child', who learn that a modicum of safety and attachment can be gained by becoming the helpful and compliant servants of their parents. They are usually the children of at least one narcissistic parent who uses contempt to press them into service-scaring and shaming them out of developing a healthy sense of self: an egoic locus of self-protection, self-care and self-compassion.*" (Excerpts are from the book, *Complex PTSD: From Thriving to Surviving* by Pete Walker)

What little Dana didn't know was that silence didn't save her. Silence didn't protect her. Most certainly, silence wouldn't help her heal trauma wounds, nor narcissistic abuse.

Instead, being a people-pleaser, a good girl, and keeping peace would someday turn into full blown Complex PTSD for me. Because sooner or later, our trauma is going to rear its ugly head with a vengeance.

We cannot outrun our past trauma. We can't bury it and think that we will be fine. We cannot skip the essential stage of processing, accepting, and doing the hard, yet necessary trauma recovery work.

There's a body-mind connection. Trauma can manifest itself into chronic physical pain, cancer, inflammation, auto-immune conditions, depression, anxiety, PTSD, Complex PTSD, addictions, and ongoing medical conditions.

According to Babette Rothschild, author of *The Body Remembers: The Psychophysiology of Trauma and Trauma Treatment,* states, "*In PTSD a traumatic event is not remembered and relegated to one's past in the same way as other life events. Trauma continues to intrude with visual, auditory, and/or other somatic reality on the lives of its victims. Again and again, they relive the life-threatening experiences they suffered, reacting in mind and body as though such events were still occurring. PTSD is a complex psychobiological condition.*"

From the Twilight Zone to Crystal Clarity

After 57 years of living with trauma and Complex PTSD, here is what I've learned. Those who are in the midst of a toxic relationship cannot clearly see it. Not in the initial stages. They're so entrenched in the unhealthy attachment that they can't see the destruction it caused. The only way to fully grasp the severity is to separate yourself from it.

More than anything, I wish that I knew three decades ago what I know now. I wish that I would have been able to understand child abuse, sexual assaults, narcissistic abuse, sibling abuse, and the dysfunctional family unit. Back then, I never heard of narcissistic abuse, narcissistic personality disorder, gaslighting, or stonewalling. Sometimes, we must give ourselves an extra dose of grace. We do not know what we don't know.

It was not until September 2017 when the fog slowly lifted. When I awoke from this trancelike state. When I became alert with lucidity. With my eyes wide opened, I found myself shocked and unsettled. My reality left me filled with despair. Everything became crystal clear. Being in my mother's presence made me physically ill.

Though I loved my mom dearly, I could not be in a relationship with her anymore. The ongoing psychological abuse hurt too much. After all of these years, I suffered the toll of narcissistic abuse, child abuse, CPTSD, and compounded trauma.

Horrified, I read through my journals. Stacks of countless journals with tell-tale signs. As the tears slipped down my face, I noticed a pattern. There were red flags flying! They alerted me and screamed for my attention.

The gaslighting. Controlling. Denial. Deception. Conflicts. Invalidation. Betrayal. Retaliation. Gossiping. Outright malicious lies. Hoovering. Provoking me. Recruiting my toxic sisters as flying monkeys to do her dirty work. Selective amnesia about what she said and did to me. The blame games. Triangulating my relationships with my dad, siblings, relatives, husband, and my children.

My journal revealed that each time I had been with my mom, I'd end up very sick. Following each visit, I had suffered excruciating migraines, nausea, vomiting, vertigo, intense insomnia, depression, and anxiety. My fibromyalgia and backpain would flare-up.

By July 2018, I could no longer ignore these clear signs. I couldn't minimize it. I could not pretend that everything was fine. Regardless of how difficult it was, I knew what I had to do. My decision was not impulsive, nor done lightly.

Instead, it took me years to finally reach this turning point. After exhausting all efforts, no contact was my last resort. A defining moment in time to walk away from my entire dysfunctional family of origin. To find my way out of the fog. To listen to the soft voice inside of me. To trust my gut instincts. To know my intuition always has my best interests at heart.

To detox from the codependency with my mother. To break free from our toxic relationship. To cut the final ties to her. To have the courage to love myself enough that I would let go of the woman who wasn't capable to give me the unconditional love that I am worthy of.

TWO

The Cunning Masquerade

"In order to lure people into their web and get this narcissistic supply, they put on an attractive social mask."

Patricia Armesto Corral

To understand a narcissist and their cunning tricks, it's important to educate ourselves about who they truly are. To look beyond their masquerade. In this chapter, we will take a deep dive into the psychology of a narcissist.

The narcissist is quite clever. They conceal their true identity. They are masters at pretending to be someone who they are not. In the early stages of a relationship with a narcissist, especially when dating, they will appear attentive to you.

At first, you may think they are charming, charismatic, and kindhearted. They may shower you with gifts, compliments, and praises. During the beginning, they will be there for you to comfort you, to support you, and to listen to you.

Do not be fooled. It's a devious act. The narcissist is such an expert at fooling people; hook, line, and sinker! They are so good at playing 'make-believe,' they could win a Hollywood Oscar for best actor or actress.

The narcissist is terrified of being exposed. This stems from their childhood wounds, fears, and inability to be transparent. They lack empathy, integrity, honesty, and authenticity. Underneath their false bravado, they are insecure cowards.

According to the DSM-5, the Diagnostic and Statistical Manual of Mental Disorders, Narcissistic Personality Disorder (NPD) is defined as, *"A personality disorder with a long-term pattern of abnormal behavior characterized by exaggerated feelings of self-importance, an excessive need for admiration, and a lack of empathy. People affected by it often spend a lot of time thinking about achieving power or success, or about their appearance. They often take advantage of the people around them. The behavior typically begins by early adulthood, and occurs across a variety of social situations."*

The Mayo Clinic defines NPD as, *"Narcissistic personality disorder — one of several types of personality disorders — is a mental condition in which people have an inflated sense of their own importance, a deep need for excessive attention and admiration, troubled relationships, and a lack of empathy for others. But behind this mask of extreme confidence lies a fragile self-esteem that's vulnerable to the slightest criticism."*

Narcissistic personality disorder (NPD) causes problems in many areas of life, such as relationships, work, school or financial affairs. People with NPD may be generally unhappy and disappointed when they're not given the special favors or admiration, which they believe they deserve. They may find their relationships unfulfilling. Others may not enjoy being around them.

Have you questioned if your family member, intimate partner, or spouse is a narcissist? Are you feeling as if you are losing your mind? If so, here's a list of signs and symptoms of narcissistic personality disorder. People with this disorder may:

- Have a ginormous ego
- Crave to be the center of attention
- Have an exaggerated sense of self-importance
- Have a sense of entitlement
- Desire excessive admiration
- Believe they are superior to everyone else
- Tear others down in order to puff themselves up
- Expect to be highly praised & recognized without achievements to warrant it
- Take advantage of others to get what they want
- Have traits of a pathological liar
- Have an inability to recognize the needs & feelings of others
- Have sinister motives
- Be envious of others
- Not living in their conscious reality
- Inflict harm on others without any guilt, shame, or remorse
- Be arrogant, haughty, & boastful
- Have a domineering & aggressive personality
- Be a control freak who abuses their power
- Expect the scapegoat to be compliant, cooperative, & submissive
- Have cruel words, actions, & behaviors

The Narcissists' Jekyll & Hyde Persona

The malignant narcissist has a split persona. They are like Jekyll and Hyde. One minute, they are sweet as sugar. The next minute, they fly into an uncontrollable seething rage! The narcissist loves playing mind games with you. They are clever to conceal who they are. Wherever there's a narcissist, you can find a false mask plastered upon their face.

Up until my early forties, I didn't realize that my own mother was a narcissist. During this time, I didn't connect the dots. I felt perplexed. Her words, behaviors, and actions had significant discrepancies. Despite her claiming to love me, her evil actions proved otherwise.

I will never forget the evening when my daughter's and I had dinner at my mom's home. It was August 2006 when we finished eating a delicious meal. Following supper, my daughters ventured off to play, while I helped my mom to clean her kitchen.

As I opened the refrigerator door to place the dishes inside, I could see out of the corner of my eye a bizarre look on my mom's face. Her expression was extreme fury. It made no logical sense. Silenty, I thought, *"What in the world's going on with her?"*

Puzzled, I didn't understand how she could abruptly shift from being happy to flying into a frenzy. In the blink of an eye, she went from calm to being furious. What brought this on? We were simply tidying up her kitchen. I never said or did anything to provoke her. As I closed the refrigerator door, I looked at my mother and said, *"What's wrong?"*

My mom charged over to me, screaming and cussing at me. Unexpectedly, she flung her hand out to slap me in the face. Before she could physically assault me, I quickly stepped back. I raised my hands in the air, blurting, *"Hell no! You will not put a hand onto me."*

Promptly, I marched into the TV room, asked my girls to gather their toys, and we drove off into the night. For days after this disturbing event, I didn't contact my mother. Something inside of me knew intuitively that she was mentally unstable. It upset me that I couldn't trust or feel safe around my own mother. I could no longer unsee the horrifying things she said and did to me.

A week later, my mother contacted me by phone. She acted as if her Jekyll & Hyde incident didn't happen. She behaved friendly and cheerful, inviting to take me out to lunch. She let on as if everything were rosy between us.

No matter how troublesome this situation felt, a part of me wanted to trust her. I wanted to believe that she didn't mean to hurt me. I desperately hoped that my mom would treat me better. Over and over, I fell for her masquerade. Hook, line, and sinker!

Looking back, I now understand why it's so hard to leave a narcissist. I now know why it's incredibly excruciating to accept that our loved one is a narcissist. Because the truth hurts. The truth runs deep. The truth cuts like a knife. If we are not willing to accept the truth, it will hold us captive. It will keep us in bondage. And the cycle of abuse will continue on.

Myths about Mothers

Our society has a twisted sense of motherhood. They believe that all mothers are kind, tender, gentle, and loving. Unfortunately, not all women who give birth to children are a good parent. Not all women are fit to be mothers.

Just because someone gave birth to you doesn't mean they are capable of caring for you. Just because a woman had a child doesn't necessarily equate to being safe, respectful, or healthy. NOT ALL MOTHERS CAN LOVE.

Most certainly, the narcissistic mother cannot give her child unconditional love. She's not capable of being self-less, devoted, warm, mature, or attentive to you. Instead, everything is about her. Life revolves around meeting her unrealistic, immature needs.

She expects your undivided attention. Your admiration. Your praises. Your loyalty to her. She demands you to meet her needs no matter how ridiculous they can be.

The narcissistic mother is a lethal force to reckon with. If you don't give her the flattery she craves, she will lash out at you like a rattlesnake. Unraveling, she has an emotional meltdown. She flies into a frenzy, shouting at you, bullying you, gaslighting you, and manipulating you. If she's anything like my mother, she will victim-blame you with F-bombs flying!

One of the challenges adult children of narcissistic mother's face is the myth that every mother is giving, nurturing, and gracious. Worldwide, this is a false notion and taboo topic. For many adult children, they are scolded by our society who chides, *"But it's your MOTHER!"*

Despite the fact that we've spent a lifetime suffering chronic mental abuse, rejection, criticisms, and scapegoating by our mothers, most people don't believe us, don't understand us, nor have they personally experienced narcissistic abuse by their mothers.

No doubt, this is what keeps us silent for decades. We become isolated and alone. We are blamed for our mother's neglect and abuse. People refuse to believe that mothers can be toxic. We don't discuss it because we grow weary of naysayers accusing us of being 'bad people,' that we 'imagined it,' or we 'must honor thy parent.'

One of the trademarks of a narcissistic parent is they have a limited capacity to feel empathy. Most don't feel empathic at all. They don't care about how their children feel, nor do they care about their kid's basic needs, such as nutrition, shelter, clothing, medicine, healthcare, appropriate education, and safety.

Narcissistic mothers are only concerned with how the rest of society views them. All eyes must be on them; not on their children. Darlene Lancer, JD, MFT, a licensed therapist and expert on codependency, sums up the facts of a narcissistic mother. This applies to narcissistic fathers, too.

On PsychologyToday.com, Lancer states, *"Our mother is our first love. She is our introduction to life and to ourselves. She is our lifeline to security. We initially learn about ourselves and our world through interactions with her. We naturally long for her physical and emotional sustenance, her touch, her smile, and her protection. Her empathetic reflection of our feelings, wants, and needs informs us who we are and that we have value. A narcissistic mother who cannot empathize damages her children's healthy psychological development. Like Narcissus in the Greek myth, she sees only a reflection of herself. There is no boundary of separateness between her and her children, whom she cannot see as unique individuals worthy of love. Symptoms of narcissism that make up narcissistic personality disorder (NPD) vary in severity, but they inevitably compromise a narcissist's ability to parent."*

Recovering from the trauma inflicted by our narcissistic mother (or father/spouse/partner) takes time and effort. For some, it can take decades to understand, process, and unpack it. Healing isn't a marathon. Rather, it's a daily journey. We gain more insight. We educate ourselves. We process our painful abuse. We know that we are worthy of being loved, respected, and cared for.

Signs You Have a Narcissistic Mother: (This applies to most narcissistic relationships.)

1. The Narcissistic Mother Lack's Boundaries – Whether you are a man or woman, your mother does not respect you, nor your boundaries. At the drop of a hat, she expects you to stop everything and come to her rescue. Even if you are at work. She will publicly criticize you, harshly judge you, and humiliate you on purpose. If you go grey rock or no contact with her, she will disregard it and trample all over your clear boundaries. She will repeatedly contact you by phone, mail, text messages, social media, and/or use other people to gain access to you.

2. The Narcissistic Mother is Emotionally Unavailable – Through your childhood to your adulthood, your mom is not emotionally available for you. She may have been physically present, yet she was cold, distant, or distracted by her own life. Despite your yearning for her comfort, attention, and affection, she is aloof. When you may have gone to her for advice, to talk about your troubles, or concerns, she harshly scolded you for being difficult. She may have hissed, *"Get over it! Stop talking about it."* You've come to realize that something is vitally missing from your relationship with her.

3. The Narcissistic Mother is overly Controlling – Your mother controls you, controls how you look, what you wear, what you say, what you believe, your health, your emotional wellbeing, how you decorate your own home, the job you have, what you eat, and how you live your life. She will make extreme attempts to control not only you, but also your intimate partner, spouse, children, grandchildren, friends, and even your pets. No matter what you choose, what you say, or what you do, she will undermine you. When your mom can no longer control you, she will try to control how other's see you and what they think about you. This goes hand in hand with her manipulative tactics in triangulating each of your relationships. She aims to destroy you and your relationships with other people, including your own siblings, parent, children, spouse, and/or intimate partner.

4. The Narcissistic Mother Dumps Toxic Shame onto Her Children – According to WebMD.com, "*Toxic shame is a feeling that you're worthless. It happens when other people treat you poorly and you turn that treatment into a belief about yourself. You're most vulnerable to this type of poor treatment during childhood or as a teen. When you feel toxic shame, you see yourself as useless or, at best, not as good as others.*" Your mom may have used guilt tactics, stonewalling, manipulation, and projection to dump toxic shame onto you. The false guilt tells you, "*What you did is wrong. You are a bad person.*" If you were raised as child by a narcissistic mom, you may have spent a lifetime being mistreated and shamed for things that you never did. Toxic shame is a result of being told you are not enough. You may feel worthless and unlovable.

5. The Narcissistic Mother is Self-Absorbed – Whether you are young or old, your mom may have been self-involved. She thinks life revolves around her. She may have not attended your PTA meetings when you were in school. She may not have showed up for anything pertaining to your educational pursuits, including when you graduated from high school or college. My own mom skipped my sister's high school graduation. Instead, she stayed home and became intoxicated with alcohol. When I graduated from beauty school and medical school, my mother refused to attend my special events. During my childhood and teen years, my mom spent most of her time at work, with her friends, bar hopping, and jumping into one destructive relationship after another. I spent my childhood unsupervised and neglected by my mother. In your case, your mother may be a workaholic, a shopaholic, an alcoholic, a pill popper, or consumed in her life. Your mother's motto may be, *"It's my way or the highway!"*

6. The Narcissistic Mother is Highly Competitive – Due to her insecurities, intense need for praise, and her lack of self-esteem, your mother will compete with you. She will try to outdo you. She will compete with your appearance. She may compete to her long list of admirers with you, accusing you of not being "slim enough, pretty enough, smart enough, or handsome enough." She can compete with you in the workplace, with money, materialism, and with objects, such as her car, home, jewelry, and her high-end designer fashion to boost her inflated ego. In my case, my mom became furious when I started growing my author and speaker platform. Following my public speaking event in 2018, which was the hallmark of my speaking career earning excellent income, my mom blasted nasty remarks to me. She acted ticked off that my career was going well. She complained, *"When will you get a REAL job?"* This resulted in her hurting me for my awesome accomplishments. She intentionally excluded me from family functions. She gossiped to my siblings about me. And she called me on the phone screaming profanities.

The trauma recovery with a narcissistic mother (or father) is not an easy one. There may be bumps in the road. You may have grown up feeling rejected, ostracized, or condemned. You may have moments when your inner critic screamed awful words to you.

Essentially, healing means you must release codependent relationships with toxic folks. It starts by identifying and understanding the shameful messages and beliefs that were transferred from the perpetrators to you, which are false. In effort to heal your mother wound (or father wound), it requires you to replace the negative, internalized messages to be transformed into positive self-talk that is kind, loving, nurturing, and respectful.

The Silver Lining

After suffering years of narcissistic abuse, there is a silver lining. According to Free Dictionary, *"A silver lining is the potential for something positive or beneficial to result from a negative situation."*

Here is our silver lining…

One day, we wake up to the narcissist's cunning masquerade. We watch their fake mask slip off their face. Everything becomes crystal clear. We see right through their phony disguise.

To anyone who's dealt with the pain and torment of a narcissist, a silver lining is a sign of hope. Hope that someday you can break free from the abuse. Hope to rebuild a better life. Hope to find comfort and peace within. Hope to recover from your trauma. Hope to embrace a brighter future.

We can no longer unsee their hideous charade. We accept how lethal a malignant narcissist is. We actively set healthy boundaries. We walk away from hurtful relationships. Like the Phoenix, we rise above the fiery ashes. We stand up, dust ourselves off, and march forward.

THREE

Roles of the Toxic Family Unit

"Children who are scapegoated in families are in reality victims of abuse and neglect – Yet this is rarely recognized by those working in our Mental Health systems, Family Courts, or Educational systems. Because scapegoating processes can be subtle, many scapegoated adult survivors fail to realize that they have suffered from psycho-emotional abuse growing up, and even their therapist or counselor might miss the signs and symptoms associated with being in this most devastating dysfunctional family role."

Rebecca C. Mandeville

I grew up in a dysfunctional family. Although I was aware of the unhealthy dynamics, I didn't grasp how perverse it was, until July 2018. Out of nowhere, I observed that my siblings and I took on clear roles in our toxic family unit. I had spent five decades feeling baffled and unsettled by the harmful patterns.

It's perplexing how family members claim their undying love for us. They can say whatever they choose, but their actions and behaviors don't match their words. There is an imbalance in the relationships with distinct discrepancies, especially in who overpowers the scapegoat.

Meanwhile, we go through the motions robotically. We attend family gatherings on birthdays, holidays, weddings, and Mother's Day. We shower our family with praises and gifts of adoration. We slip back into our unhealthy roles repeatedly as if we were a broken record. We are oblivious to our destructive family habits. We're consumed in turmoil. We can feel as if we're slowly dying.

Somehow, we lost our core selves along our uphill battle. We abandoned our own selves. After surviving neglect and abuse, we've become drained and exhausted. We have forgotten who we are with our amazing traits, strengths, and talents. We mostly see ourselves in the role as the helpless, ostracized family scapegoat. Or the black sheep of the toxic family unit.

Our self-identity became enmeshed into decades of a web of lies that we were told. The deception was a part of brainwashing. The lies shrieked, *"You are bad. You are to blame. You should be ashamed of yourself. You are powerless!"*

On the website, TheMadTherapy.com, they shared components of a narcissistic family. *"All families have roles in which each member acts in accordance. However, in narcissistic families the roles are distinct and damaging to the members individually as well as the family unit. The roles continue the level of dysfunction within the family unit with the purpose being to protect the narcissist from addressing their own unresolved issues with themselves or others. Thus, how family roles are assigned are intentional, discretely assigned to each member and can go unnoticed for years due to the dysfunctional dynamics and abuse tactics."*

In effort to unravel this mystery, we must learn each of the family roles. Knowledge is powerful. It can equip us with insight to understand how we fell into the scapegoat role. We can discover facts and educate ourselves. We can dismantle our family role. We may choose to no longer participate as the scapegoat or black sheep of the family. We can reclaim our true identity. We can rescue our own souls.

In this chapter, I will explain what each of the family roles can look like. It may help you to identify them in your own family and/or narcissistic relationships. Once we can pinpoint what role we and others play, we can start to be intentional in breaking free of our toxic roles. Most essential of all, we can start to heal our trauma.

Six Dysfunctional Family Roles:

1. The Narcissist – Oftentimes, it's your father, mother, or stepparent. It can also be a grandparent, sibling, and/or relative. A narcissistic father emotionally damages their children. They disregard their boundaries, are manipulative, withhold affection from their children (until the child performs), and they neglect the emotional needs of their children because they're most interested in having their own needs met. There is profound tension amongst the family members who are ruled by a tyrannical narcissistic father. In many of these families, the mother simply echoes the father as she feels uncertain of herself (due to his emotional abuse) and is afraid to confront her spouse. This destructive pattern is the result of the mother's own traumatic childhood. A narcissistic mother thinks she's Queen of the household. You follow her absurd demands or else you are doomed to punishment. The narcissistic mother is domineering, emotionally immature, and vindictive. There's a saying that when mama isn't happy than nobody is happy. In this toxic family, everyone is miserable. When the narc mom doesn't get her own way, she will have a hissy fit, scream obscenities, and throw objects across the room like a toddler. A narcissistic mom can act like two entirely different people; Jekyll and Hyde persona. When nobody is looking, the narcissistic mother is cruel, dismissive, and/or detached. When the narc mom is out in public, she's friendly, bragging about your accomplishments, or acting lovingly towards you. Unfortunately, it's a façade. Behind her false pretense is an egotistical dictator who oppresses each family member, including you.

2. The Enabling Parent – This person is your mother, father, or a stepparent. They may be married or divorced to their narcissistic spouse. The enabling parent is overpowered by their narcissistic husband, wife, or ex-spouse. Their world revolves around keeping peace with the narcissist. The fall for every single lie, manipulation, and covert scheme. It's like they are under the narcissist's spell. Due to the enabler being hyper-focused on the narc, they are emotionally absent from their children. The enabling mother or father of a narcissistic parent is a secondary abuser. They don't rescue their child/children from the nonstop mental and/or physical torture. The lack of parental support to the child can suggest the enabling parent's needs are more important to the parent than their child's basic needs. Is it any wonder why the entire family unit crumbles?

3. The Golden Child – This person is usually one of the siblings or step children within a broken family. It could be your brother, sister, or the step sibling. The golden child becomes designated for all of the family's successes. This child tends to be exceptional in one or more ways (physically beautiful, charming nature, intelligent, athletic, or talented), and the family uses this asset as leverage for appearing superior to our society. Therefore, he or she is the embodiment of perfection. The golden child is the special child who's a projection of all the impeccable traits of the narcissist. The golden child is an extension of the narcissistic dad or mom. Even when the golden child sees the negative flaws of the narc parent, they stay loyal and devoted to them. At all costs, they will protect and defend the narcissist. Everything they touch turns to gold. He or she may be the star of their class, adored by everyone, and considered a brilliant person.

4. The Forgotten Child – This is one or more of your siblings. The forgotten child is meek, shy, and passive. They may be an introvert. In their submissive nature, they willingly give away their power. They bow down to the narcissistic parent, golden child, and the family bully. The forgotten child is actually the 'lost child' who the toxic family doesn't notice. The lost child falls through the cracks within their own fractured family system. Some forgotten children grow up to become traumatized adults. As teens and adults, they may seek out ways to numb their pain by addictive behaviors, including addictions to food, alcohol, drugs, sex, shopping, gambling, and/or people-pleasing. Typically, they live in denial of their trauma, dysfunctional family, and addictions as well as their family role. It directly leads to their loyalty to the golden child, narcissist, and family bully. Due to their pain, insecurities, and weaknesses, they betray the scapegoat in order to remain intact within the dysfunctional family unit. For the forgotten child, it's all about 'saving face' to avoid family disgrace, humiliation, and ostracization.

5. The Family Bully – This person is usually one of your aggressive siblings. They are a hostile bully and control freak. The family bully takes sibling rivalry to a whole new level; sibling abuse. While it's common for families to have sibling rivalry, what stands out the most with the bully is their intent to hurt others badly, especially the family scapegoat. They can physically harm you. They will mentally torture you. In some cases, they will sexually violate you. They have evil motives to control their family members, manipulate them, and gaslight them. The family bully tries to influence each family member. They'll do it covertly; not directly because they don't want to get caught. They relish in provoking family conflicts, division, and animosity. Then they slyly step back to watch the entire family explode, all while playing innocent. The family bully is the first one to shift the blame to the scapegoat. As an adult, the bully creatively manipulates both parents to include them in the family will, inheritance, and they play favorites to the enabling parent. The family bully will butt heads with the narcissistic parent and spend a lifetime in heated conflicts with them. Ironically, the bully will not blink an eye when they ruthlessly steal the family trust fund right out from under their scapegoat sibling. The bully is heartless, mentally unstable, and quite lethal. Sometimes they masquerade as a sheep of the family or pretend to be a 'good Christian.' Don't be fooled! They're a ravenous wolf who is predatory, menacing, and greedy. They prey on the family scapegoat and try to overpower you. When you least expect it, they will not only betray you and your trust, but they'll have a grin upon their face when they kick you under the bus.

6. The Family Scapegoat – According to MindFool.com, "*The word family scapegoat comes from an ancient Jewish tradition where a goat was sent to the wilderness to compensate and atone for the sins, misdeeds, and immoral acts of the community people. In family scapegoating, a narcissistic or abusive parent blames a single person, especially a child for whatever is wrong in the family. They become the target of blame, ostracism, criticism, judgements, and disapproval.*" This true story is from the Bible in the Old Testament; Leviticus 16. "*Aaron is to offer the bull for his own sin offering to make atonement for himself and his household. Then he is to take the two goats and present them before the Lord at the entrance to the tent of meeting. He is to cast lots for the two goats—one lot for the Lord and the other for the scapegoat. Aaron shall bring the goat whose lot falls to the Lord and sacrifice it for a sin offering. But the goat chosen by lot as the scapegoat shall be presented alive before the Lord to be used for making atonement by sending it into the wilderness as a scapegoat.*" (Leviticus 16:6-10 NIV)

In a similar way, all other members of a negative familial feel better (or free from their sins) after dumping their issues on one family member—the scapegoat. Usually, the black sheep or family scapegoat is the smartest, kindest, healthiest, strongest, and wisest person of the family. This also means that other family members subconsciously are fearful of this person's potential and power. Therefore, they want to suppress the scapegoat. This can be done in many ways. It's commonly achieved by making him or her believe that they are not good enough or they lack positive traits. When this is done to a person at a young age, it leaves a painful imprint on their minds. This can lead them to believe that they deserve nothing good, which results in a low self-esteem, a lack of self-love, and lifelong challenges in relationships. In simple terms, a scapegoat is the family punching bag. On a daily basis, you are singled out for all the collective ridicule, made into the butt of every joke, and excluded from family events, holidays, and important legal family matters. It doesn't take long for outsiders or other relatives to take note of your role and to be drawn into the destructive dynamics. Family scapegoats are belittled, humiliated, battered, rejected, betrayed, and treated poorly. It's a clear case of psychological abuse, manipulation, and bullying.

In *Complex PTSD: From Surviving to Thriving* by Pete Walker, an abuse survivor, licensed psychotherapist, author, and trauma-informed expert, he states, *"Narcissistic and borderline parents typically choose at least one child to be the designated family scapegoat. Scapegoating is the process by which a bully off-loads and externalizes his pain, stress, and frustration by attacking a less powerful person. Scapegoating brings the bully some momentary relief. It does not however effectively metabolize or release his pain, and scapegoating soon resumes as the bully's internal discomfort resurfaces."*

Pete Walker goes on to inform, *"In especially dysfunctional families, the scapegoating parent often organizes the rest of the family to also gang up on the scapegoat. Severely narcissistic parents are rarely embarrassed by their aggressive behavior. They feel entitled to punish a child for anything that displeases them, no matter how unreasonable it might appear to an impartial observer. I believe there is an epidemic of sibling abuse that afflicts many dysfunctional families. Siblings in such families can traumatize the victim-scapegoat as severely as the parents. In families with checked out, disinterested parents, they can in fact be the chief sources of trauma."*

Your family relationships built during early developmental years determines your success in adult bonding. It sets the tone of how you are to interact with the world at large. In family scapegoating, a single person is chosen to carry the heavy burden of family guilt, secrets, anger, and frustration of the entire unit.

Common Signs of Family Scapegoating:

- **Victim-Blaming & Shaming** - A family scapegoat is burdened with criticism, toxic shame, and blame for something they have **not** done. The wrongdoings of others are projected onto them. The words, 'you're not good enough,' 'you cannot do anything right,' or 'you are the problem' are continuously fed into the person's ears. It breeds insecurity, especially when the toxic family dumps shame, self-doubt, and blame onto the scapegoat. You were a convenient receptacle for your insecure family members who were incapable or unwilling to take responsibility for their own actions, words, and behaviors.

- **Verbal Abuse** – The toxic family will lash out at you, saying, *"You're so lazy, incompetent, and stupid," "You are a difficult person to love,"* or *"You won't amount to anything."* No matter what you say or do, they insist you are the bad person in the family. You don't fit in. Your parents, siblings, or both have habitually belittled you. They call you nasty names, cuss you out, put you on a guilt trip, and verbally attack you. This is a reflection of them; not you.
- **Ignored** – You will be the last one to hear anything important that's happening within the family unit. If someone is sick, admitted into the hospital, or if someone dies, the toxic family tries to withhold this information. If there's a wedding, family dinner, or special event, you are not included. Yet, a week or two later, the narcissistic parent tells on her or his own self. They gloat about their entertaining time with all of your siblings and how much fun they had without YOU. It's another way to rub it in your face and to try to make you feel bad. Don't fall for it. This is how they bait you into arguments. One of the top reasons you are ignored is because you stand in the truth, speak the truth, and it drives your family nuts.
- **No Emotional Support** – It's common in your dysfunctional family of origin to receive little to no emotional support. When your narcissistic mother/father is sick, you are always there for her/him. When your brother had back surgery, you whipped up homemade meals for him. When your sister-in-law lost her job, you gave her money inside a card. Yet, where are they when something goes wrong in your life? Suddenly, they're missing in action. No calls. No cards. No visits. No flowers. No kind gestures. In other words, they don't care

about you. Their lake of empathy and compassion speaks loudly about their own core character; selfish, insensitive, and cold. Typically, the scapegoat will find emotional support with his or her partner, spouse, friends, or adult children. However, some scapegoats are isolated and alone. Each person may have a unique experience with emotional support or the lack of it.

- **Physical & Sexual Abuse Targets** – It is highly unfortunate that many scapegoats are targeted by each member of their family for ritual abuse. It can be domestic violence, physical assault, and or sexual assault. In my own case, my sister's husband sexually assaulted me in 2006. When I informed my sister about what happened, she victim-blamed me, saying, *"You asked for it! This is your fault. Be a good Christian and forgive him fast."* Ultimately, my birth family had the motto, *"Just get over it! Move on."* The fact about sexual trauma (or any form of trauma) is that survivors do **not** just get over it. We cannot move on. We don't need to pray harder, forgive fast, nor justify a legal crime. We were violated! Our traumatic events stay with us; cellular memory is within our entire body. Even if we could forget about it, our body remembers the violation. Our body and each cell inside will never forget it. *"Traumatized people chronically feel unsafe inside their bodies: The past is alive in the form of gnawing interior discomfort. Their bodies are constantly bombarded by visceral warning signs, and, in an attempt to control these processes, they often become expert at ignoring their gut feelings and in numbing awareness of what is played out inside. They learn to hide from their selves."* ~ Bessel A. van der Kolk, The Body Keeps the Score: Brain, Mind, and Body in the Healing of Trauma
- **False Accusations** – Oftentimes, you find yourself being accused of false accusations. For example, you could be in the midst of cooking dinner or folding laundry while a family member who's lounging on the sofa as they watch TV accuses you of being lazy. Clearly, this is not true. They are describing themselves and projecting their own self-hate onto you.

- **You're the Family Doormat** – Your parents and siblings walk all over you as if you are their doormat. If your sister's not feeling well, you get punished for it. She randomly screams at you and creates drama. When your dad had a hard day at work, he not only arrives home grumpy, but he takes it out on you. Despite how much you do to support other family members and pitch in to help, they take advantage of you, they don't appreciate you, and they mistreat you.
- **Triangulation of Relationships** – According to OvercomingToxicPeople.com, "*Triangulation is a tactic used by narcissist family members to devastating effect. I've seen how harmful it can be in relationships between mothers, fathers, brothers, and sisters. Triangulation is a form of abuse where a narcissist either puts themselves between two family members to control the dynamic or attacks a victim indirectly through a third party.*" In families, narcissistic triangulation is a common way where the narcissist, typically a parent, controls, manipulates, and gaslights other family members, especially the scapegoat. The toxic family unit seeks masterful ways to destroy your relationships with your own mother, father, grandparents, siblings, relatives, your friendships, your marriage or intimate partnership, and/or relationship with your own children.

Positive Traits of a Scapegoat

What the toxic family unit has lost sight of is the positive traits of the innocent person who was manipulated into being the scapegoat. The scapegoat can feel the acute injustice that leaves a psychological scar. Although nobody would willingly choose to be a scapegoat, this person has countless wonderful strengths, characteristics, and accomplishments.

Top Traits of a Scapegoat:

- Truth Seekers
- Empathic
- Compassionate
- Free thinkers
- Old souls
- They care about & fight for justice
- Highly Sensitive People
- Unique and nothing like their siblings or parents
- Creative
- They look outside the box
- Whistle blowers
- Authentic
- Courageous
- Transparent
- Empowered
- Intuitive nature
- Fearless
- Unstoppable
- Healers
- Loving caretakers

Do you have any of the positive traits of a scapegoat? Can you identify with your scapegoat role? What about your family members' roles? Once we understand what these family roles are and where our place is in it, it is usually pretty clear to identify who plays what role. It also helps us to understand how the family dysfunction continues if we remain in a relationship with one or more abusive family members.

As hurtful and damaging as family scapegoating is, you can learn to reprogram the dialogue in your head that tells you, *"You're going to fail, you can't do it, you're not good enough."* Those are blatant lies from the inner critic. Please don't beat yourself up over it.

Understand that it's part of your trauma recovery. Through time, you can silence your inner critic. You can learn new skills to cope. You can gain more education, knowledge, and tools about how to manage your symptoms of trauma. You can affirm daily that you are divinely loved and supported. Helpful strategies and healing modalities are in upcoming chapters and in the professional resources.

The truth is, you can do anything you put your mind to. You can succeed. You can learn something brand new. You can start a wonderful new season of life. You can transform your subconscious mind to become healthy, optimistic, and positive. You are good enough just as you are. If you're willing to be vigilant, put in the effort, and do the healing work, you can live a healthy, rewarding, happy, and fulfilling life.

FOUR

When the Fog Lifts

"As you recover, you will feel more conscious of your surroundings. Freed from the 'fog' of your pain, fear, and confusion, you will awaken and see the world revealed as never before."

Author unknown

In 2017, I started to see things that I hadn't noticed before about my birth family. Gradually, month by month, there was a shift. At first, it was subtle. During interactions with my siblings and mother, I observed odd words, actions, and behaviors from them. I continually caught them red-handed in blatant lies.

When I confronted them, they had 'selective amnesia.' How convenient of them to randomly forget what they had said and done to me. Selective amnesia by the narcissist and flying monkeys is when the real crazy-making three ring circus reaches toxic proportions.

My abusive siblings and mom innocently objected, *"I don't' know what you're talking about," "I don't recall doing that," "It's your imagination,"* or *"You must be confused."*

No, we know exactly what we're talking about. We know precisely what happened. We clearly understand what they said and did. It's not our wild imagination. We are not confused. We're not the crazy ones!

Actually, when the fog lifts everything becomes crystal clear. It's when we have a light bulb AHA moment. We comprehend our conscious reality. We can no longer unsee the harrowing, unspeakable things that our family, spouse, partner, or ex did to us.

Selective amnesia by harmful people is blame-shifting. According to FreeDictionary.com, *"Blame-shifting is when someone shifts the blame from person to person."* The root of blame-shifting is when an abusive person fails to take responsibility for their cruelty.

It's a manipulative tactic to take the attention off of them by accusing us of being the problem. Blame-shifting is when a person does something inappropriate and they dump the blame onto someone else. They avoid taking accountability for their own revolting words, actions, and behaviors.

Signs of Blame-shifting:

- **Play the 'Victim Card'** – The narcissist and flying monkeys twist your words. They take a half truth and spin it into a web of lies. For example, you might ask your narcissistic ex-spouse to stop ridiculing you. Since the situation paints you as a victim, they are quick to turn the tables. They pretend they're the victim and you are the bad guy. Rather than they own up to their deceit, they choose to deny it and continue deceiving you. They cry, *"Poor me. I'm the one suffering,"* during their pity party. Instead of the toxic person addressing your legitimate concerns, they bring up or fabricate stories about something completely unrelated to the topic of discussion. They are merely back-peddling. It's another attempt to try to wiggle their way out of the fact that you caught them in lies.
- **Minimize the Facts** – After the fog lifts and you awaken to

the truth about abuse, the narcissist and flying monkeys will minimize the facts about what took place. They will discredit you. They will undermine your own perception. They will accuse you of being insane. Even if you took the time to explain yourself, they will cast all blame onto you. If you communicate to them how much they've hurt you, they will laugh at you and jokingly say, "*Something is wrong with you. Perhaps, you need to see a shrink?*" Or they will dismiss your valid emotions and concerns by snickering, "*You need help,*" "*You are too sensitive,*" or "*Calm down!*" The blame is no longer on them for misbehaving, but on you for reacting to their misbehavior. Ironically, if you ever criticize a toxic person the way they regularly criticize you, they will freak out, become enraged, and verbally attack you.

- **Denial & Deceit** – When a person, such as the narcissist denies the facts of their despicable behaviors, they will go to extremes to deceive you. They are dishonest and will mislead you. Why do narcissists lie? As the cliché goes, because they can. Seriously, many narcissists do lie and they lie constantly. They lie about their education, they lie about their achievements, and they lie about extramarital affairs. Most importantly, they will lie about how they have abused you, hurt you, and intentionally inflicted pain onto you.
- **Lame Justification** – Just when we wonder how low can the narcissist go, they stoop even lower. Despite their nonstop cruelty, they will create lame justifications for their hideous actions and behaviors. For example, they may rant, "*Well, it's your fault because you quit calling me,*" "*I only did that because you ticked me off,*" "*Why can't you love me like everyone else? Just let it go!*" "*I have no need to apologize. You're just intolerant!*" Or "*You are nothing without me!*"
- **Guilt-Tripping** – Another bag of tricks is guilt-tripping the scapegoat. This clever act is how they manipulate you and gaslight you. It's crucial that you keep in the forefront of your mind that when you are dealing with an abusive person, they

have a very different conscience than you. The manipulator has no conscience. They are immoral. They're deliberately using your conscience against you when they use guilt-tripping. Their banking on you feeling guilty for things you have never done. They are keenly aware that you have a sound mind. They play mind-games with you and your good conscience.

- **Escalated Arguments** – When a narcissist and flying monkeys see that you are onto their sly tricks, they will argue with you. This is their final attempt to find a way out of getting caught. No matter how much they scream, cuss, and fight with you, their arguments are to trip you up. They want to provoke you into more conflicts. Remember, they crave narcissistic supply. This is why they are projecting and gaslighting you. They need you to have a negative emotional reaction to them. It feeds the fuel with them. Don't participate in the drama, denial, and dysfunction. Walk away.

When you come out of the fog, your healing journey can be accelerated. One by one, you connect the pieces of the puzzle. You begin to see the gaslighting, manipulation, and bullying for what it truly is; psychological abuse.

Gaslighting & Manipulation

Two elements of blame-shifting include gaslighting and manipulation. According to Dr. Robin Stern, the author of the book, *The Gaslight Effect, "Gaslighting is the systemic attempt by one person to erode another person's reality by telling them that what they have experienced isn't so- and the gradual giving up on the part of the person."*

Gaslighting is a subtle form of emotional manipulation that often results in the recipient doubting their own perception of reality and their sanity. In addition, gaslighting is a method of manipulation by toxic people to gain power over you. The worst part about gaslighting is that it undermines your self-worth to the point where you're second-guessing everything.

The biggest hurdle most scapegoats face is the fear of doing something wrong by going grey rock, no contact, or upsetting the narcissist if you distance yourself. You walk on eggshells. You don't feel safe. You don't know from one minute to the next how the narcissist will react to you. At any moment, they can explode!

You feel smothered. You constantly question your feelings, perceptions, and memories. A small, suffocated part inside of you wonders whether you're going crazy. This is exactly what the narcissist hopes for; that you question your mental faculties. Although you may question your emotional wellbeing and you might feel unbalanced, there is still hope.

On the website, LoneWolf.com, "*Inspired by the 1940 and 1944 films, 'Gas Light,' where a husband systematically manipulates his wife in order to make her feel crazy, the term gaslighting is now commonly used to describe behavior that is inherently manipulative. Gaslighting, at its core, is a form of emotional abuse that slowly eats away at your ability to make judgements. Essentially, a Gaslighter spins their negative, harmful or destructive words and actions in their favor, deflecting the blame for their abusive deeds and point the finger at you. This is done by making you feel 'overly sensitive,' 'paranoid,' 'mentally unstable,' 'silly,' 'unhinged,' and many other sensations which cause you to doubt yourself. Commonly adopted by psychopathic, sociopathic and narcissistic types of people, gaslighting tends to eat away at you slowly until you realize that you're a shell of the former person you were.*"

15 Subtle Signs of Gaslighting & Manipulation

1. You are accused of being paranoid, insane, & too sensitive.
2. You constantly second guess yourself.
3. Toxic people silence you.
4. The narcissist calls you irrational & a drama queen or king.

5. The toxic person accuses you of lying.
6. The narcissist & flying monkey's victim-shame & blame you.
7. The manipulator insists they're the victim & you are the perpetrator.
8. You are told that you are the problem; not them.
9. The narcissist & flying monkeys have selective amnesia.
10. The toxic folks use lame excuses to justify their spiteful actions.
11. They use religious gaslighting & scriptures as a weapon to hurt you.
12. They twist a half truth into a full-blown lie.
13. The narcissist & flying monkeys bully you, stalk you, & retaliate against you.
14. They bait you & provoke you into arguments with them.
15. Even if you have clear evidence about them bullying you, they will deny it & not take responsibility for themselves.

Healing the Wounds Ignited by Gaslighting & Manipulation

Gaslighting causes us to doubt our own memories, perceptions, and judgments. It throws us psychologically off balance. It's like being in the Twilight Zone. If you feel as though your self-esteem, confidence, and dignity has withered under the flame of gaslighting, you are not alone.

Almost all of us, including myself, have experienced gaslighting and manipulation more times than we can count. The problems arise when gaslighting and manipulation is a frequent shadow that trails behind our relationships. The good news is knowledge and awareness are the first steps to heal and rebuild a strong perception.

While it's true that in some situations we genuinely can be overreacting, or might genuinely be exhibiting irrational behavior, it is also important for you to listen to your gut. Your intuition doesn't lie.

Do you trust your intuition? Wikipedia defines intuition as, "*The ability to acquire knowledge without recourse to conscious reasoning. Different fields use the word 'intuition' in very different ways, including but not limited to: direct access to unconscious knowledge; unconscious cognition; inner sensing; inner insight to unconscious pattern-recognition; and the ability to understand something instinctively, without any need for conscious reasoning.*"

When you're dealing with a narcissist and flying monkeys, do you have a heavy feeling in the pit of your stomach? Do you feel physically ill? Do you feel weighed down, oppressed, or depressed? If so, it's signs that you have unconsciously picked up on deception and 'foul play.'

If something doesn't feel right or if something feels 'off,' learn to trust your internal warning signals. They are alerting you to danger. Some physical signs are a racing heartbeat, shortness of breath, anxiety, perspiration, a migraine, nausea, or vertigo. Your body is screaming for you to pay attention. Do not dismiss it or deny your conscious reality. Instead, learn to trust your intuition.

The JADE Technique

Are you tired of being treated like a punching bag or doormat? Are you at your wits end? Today, it's time to learn credible tools to outsmart toxic people. It can help you to increase your peace of mind and to remain calm despite the chaos going on around you. In the rest of this chapter, you will learn about the JADE technique. It's another educational strategy to help you maintain your clear boundaries.

When someone puts so much energy into blame-shifting you there's a temptation to explain yourself to them. It's normal to want to defend yourself and to prove your point. Here's the problem; this is precisely what they want you to do. It's not because they care to hear your explanation. Rather, they want you in the hot seat and squirming. They aim to discredit you.

They will intentionally dump all the blame onto you. Their motive is for you to have a meltdown. They want you crying, yelling, and swearing. They want you to lose it so they can say, *"See, I told you she or he is crazy!"*

The narcissist and flying monkeys accuse you of doing things that they're doing. They are infuriated that you caught onto them. By sucking you into conflicts and drama, they're consuming your energy, time, and watching you to see if you fall for their bait. Then they will use your emotional reactions to prove their own points by hissing, *"Wow! Look how bitter and angry you are."*

THE GOAL IS for you to not fall for their provocations. Instead, learn to practice the JADE technique. JADE is an acronym and it stands for:

J = Justify: Don't try to justify yourself to toxic people. It's unproductive.

A = Argue: Do not waste your energy arguing with toxic people.

D = Defend: Don't waste your breath trying to defend yourself to those who don't care.

E = Explain: Never explain yourself, especially to those who discredit you.

The goal of the JADE technique is to take back your power. To stand up for yourself without needing to defend or explain yourself. It's essential to not engage in this ridiculous mind-game with abusive people.

By not participating in their tactics, you can put more attention onto what matters most to you. YOU. Your life. Your health. Your sanity. Your future. Your purpose. You can focus on your healing journey. You can make positive intentions to seek comfort and to practice self-care.

FIVE

The Ruthless Discard Phase

"People who genuinely love you will not betray you, abandon you, nor discard you like trash."

Dana Arcuri, Author, Speaker, & Certified Trauma Recovery Coach

The discard phase is very subtle. In the beginning, you may accidentally miss the signs that a narcissist, flying monkeys, and/or other people have started to discard you. We don't always understand what's happening behind the scenes. One reason is because the narcissist and flying monkeys disguise themselves as sheep. Yet, they are ravaging wolves underneath this sneaky facade.

According to MariamWebster.com, *"Discard means to get rid of especially as useless or not wanted."* When someone discards you, they have rejected you. Furthermore, they don't want or need you in their life. For some survivors, this includes abusive family members (or in-laws) who cast you out of their toxic family unit as if you were trash.

If your relationship is with a narcissistic partner, spouse, or ex, it is common for them to discard you once they've replaced you by their new narcissistic supply. They may have had secret affairs behind your back, deceiving you. For months, years, or decades, you may have suspected they were cheating on you. There's a likely chance they have broken your trust, betrayed you, and have crushed your heart. Not just once, but dozens of times.

Although the discard stage can be different for each of us, there are some similarities. The discard phase typically entails gaslighting, manipulation, love bombing, hoovering, and deceit. They may have mysteriously disappeared for days, weeks, or longer. When they're missing, you can guarantee they're with their new flame; the next victim of narcissistic supply. The poor victim has no idea what they're in for!

In the case of intimate relationships and marriages, Dr. Rhonda Freeman explains the discard phase for these types of toxic relationships. She states, *"A psychopath's initial idealization or love-bombing tactics, which include grooming, manipulation, and exploitation, coupled with lying and secrets, are linked to her/his (broken) reward system of her/his brain. Without a real ability to bond with an intimate partner, the psychopath becomes easily bored and full of negative feelings about her/his partner, and sometimes, this happens without her/his partner even knowing anything is wrong. Without dialogue and an inability to discuss normal problems or issues in a relationship, the narcissist views you as an inconvenience and chooses to discard you, instead of growing in the relationship. You may be victim to her/his constant criticisms, silent devaluing of you, and her/his need for more control, but instead of realizing anything was really wrong in the relationship, you mistook his/her silent treatment as a sign that everything was okay because you're normal, and well, because adults typically outgrow the need to ignore people when they're five or six years' old."*

If it was your narcissistic parent, siblings, or relatives who discarded you, they may have reduced their communication with you. Instead of hearing from them or seeing them on a regular basis, you may notice they rarely call you, text you, or see you in person. They have nothing to do with you. If you inquire about why they have disappeared, they may deflect or avoid a discussion with you. They claim, *"I'm super busy,"* or *"I was on vacation."* They can become highly defensive, argue with you, or accuse you of avoiding them.

One of the most heartbreaking stories I heard from my coaching clients and YouTube followers is how the narcissist and/or toxic family members discarded them at the worst possible time. This can include during the loss of a job, a life-threatening medical illness, the death of their pet, or loved one, or in the midst of a major crisis.

Frequently, the devastating discard stage is during what should have been a joyous occasion, such as your anniversary, birthday, a holiday, your graduation, the birth of your baby, when you launched a new business, or right before your vacation. Sadly, you're left to pick up the broken pieces of your heart as the narcissist and/or family carries on as if nothing happened.

To you, the destructive discard seems intensely personal, callous, and appalling. As hurtful as it is, the truth is that almost all narcissists discard the people in their lives during important life events, special occasions, and soul-crushing losses. It's one of their blueprint manipulative-plans. To kick you when you are already down.

The Toxic Family Discard & Healing Father Wounds

From 2016 through 2018, my family of origin slowly discarded me. One by one, they cut me out of their lives. When my sisters went on camping trips together, they excluded me. When they went to RV shows, out to dinner, the movies, or celebrated special events, they skipped inviting me. When they took our mom out to lunch or shopping, they avoided sharing it with me.

Like clockwork, my mother called me to rub it in my face. She bragged about how her and my siblings went out together. Oh, what a good time they had without me! She'd never apologize for excluding me. She had no remorse, nor guilt for hurting me. Neither did my older sisters.

One particular situation, which stood out to me was in August 2017. It was when my four sisters planned to visit our dad out of state. They didn't inform me about it. Instead, they left me in the dark for three solid months. Everyone else knew about it, except for me.

During that timeline, I had the honor of being invited to my author friend, John Finch's, book launch team for *The Father Effect*. One perk included getting a free copy to read before the actual book release. From the first chapter, I was glued to his story. It shared John's personal journey of growing up without his dad and how it negatively influenced every facet of his life.

As I read the story of his father being emotionally absent, I related to the negative feelings of having a distant dad. Rejection. Unworthiness. Unlovable. Turning page after page, tears streamed down my face. I was blown away that someone understood my painful father wound. For the first time, I didn't feel so alone.

John's gripping message touched my heart and soul. *The Father Effect* helped me view my situation with my dad in a new perspective. I realized that my dad grew up with a father wound. His dad did, too. It may go far back to generations from long ago; intergenerational trauma.

Most fathers have a mindset dictated by our society that they're a 'good dad' if they work, provide for their family, and keep a roof over their heads. The average man doesn't know their children, young and old, crave their affection and time together. Most children yearn for their dad's love and attention. They desire a father who actively participates in their lives.

Children need their daddies. They need their father's undivided attention, affection, and adoration. After 50+ years, this had been missing in my life. It left a father wound. It hurt badly. I wasn't even aware of how it became toxic to me and everyone around me.

Through the years, it had a way of making me feel unworthy, unacceptable, and never enough. If my own flesh and blood relative wouldn't spend quality time with me or participate in my life, was I of no value? These are the hard questions we ask ourselves when our dads are missing from our lives; physically, emotionally, and spiritually.

On rare occasions when my dad visited me or contacted me, which wasn't often, it was as if this carefully placed bandage over my heart was viciously ripped off. Blood oozed everywhere. Underneath lay a festering wound. It couldn't be healed if it were not addressed or brought to light.

Suddenly, I'm that frightened little girl who's torn, confused, and hurt. She wants to run and hide. My father wound haunted me. It became a traumatic experience in my life. Despite what my mind said (move on), living without my dad wrecked me.

Year after year, my father wound snowballed out of control. I felt angry. It impacted my relationships, including with my husband. Sometimes, I lashed out at him unintentionally during moments of distress. All the while, my siblings and mom purposely triangulated my relationship with my father. They wanted to destroy it.

Although, this is no excuse, hurting people do hurt other people. When traumatized people hurt inside, they can find unhealthy, maladaptive ways to cope. While some people may turn to drugs or alcohol to dull the pain, my vice was a hardened heart. It created a wall to divide myself further from my dad.

After reading *The Father Effect,* I felt a stirring in my soul. I sensed that I needed to visit my dad to try to mend our broken relationship. I felt convicted for my negative thoughts about him. This burdened me. It struck me like a bolt of lightning.

Perhaps, it was my wake-up call to make necessary changes? For me to reexamine myself, my past, and my future. To come to terms with my unforgiveness towards my dad. To heal my father wound.

In November 2017, I received a phone call that threw me into a tizzy. My oldest sister, Becky, invited me to join her and our three siblings on a weekend getaway. They planned to celebrate Christmas early with our dad who lived out of state. A festive holiday celebration to spend time together.

The sheer idea of it sent my heart racing! Stubbornly, I told her that I wouldn't join them. Digging in my heels, I remained resistant. Still hurting with a father wound, I had a dozen logical reasons to not see my dad.

Out of nowhere something strange happened. Everything to do with forgiveness and humility crossed my path. I kid you not, it seemed like all of the songs on the radio were about healing broken relationships or humbling oneself. I'd scroll through Facebook and trip upon a post about forgiving one another. Or I'd watch shows about people mending their relationships.

Unexpectedly, God softened my heart. He even went as far as using red cardinals to pull at my heart-strings. A savvy way to grab my attention since I love cardinals. Despite being convicted, I internally wrestled with if I should see my dad or not.

One by one, my stubbornness subsided. Those rigid walls of anger and bitterness dwindled. They were replaced with empathy, compassion, and authentic love for my dad. Who can do that, but a loving Higher Power who wants us to heal trauma? This transformation was remarkable. I knew beyond a shadow of doubt, I needed to visit my father.

In December 2017, my four siblings and I headed to a Christmas gathering with our dad. Prior to our arrival, I had a lot of trepidation. My father battled advanced Alzheimer's. There was a likely chance he wouldn't remember me. What if our visit was a disappointment? What if he had negative feelings towards me, especially since I hadn't contacted him for over six months?

Once we arrived and unpacked our belongings at the hotel, we visited our dad. My heart raced with nervous energy. Silently, I prayed, "God, *I know that I made the right choice. No matter what happens may it bring You glory.*"

As my sisters and I waited for our dad to open his door, I stood behind them. Part of me felt scared of the unknown. This walk of faith truly tested me. I felt strong about doing the right thing, but it didn't mean it was easy. Actually, it was the most difficult decision for me. To lay down my will, my unforgiveness, and my years of hurt. To release my father wound.

When my dad opened his door, he welcomed us to come inside. Then he took time to give warm hugs. As he approached me, his voice filled with joy. Hugging and kissing me, he affirmed, "*Dana, I'm so glad you're here!*"

For the next two days, I walked on cloud nine. My father was a changed man. His usual business demeanor was gone. He was gentle, kind, attentive, and affectionate. Repeatedly, he'd stop what he was doing, wrap me in his arms, and tell me how much he loved me. It was music to my soul!

Out of the corner of my eye, I could see my sisters glaring at me with a stink eye. The expressions on their faces were clear. They were ticked off at me! They were outraged about my dad giving me his undivided attention and love. They didn't want my father and I restoring our relationship.

My sister scoffed, *"Dad, she's not your lover or mistress. Ewww...stop kissing and hugging her!"* Several siblings chided in agreement with her. My sister's rude remark was inappropriate. I ignored her and didn't give fuel to the fire.

During dinner, before we enjoyed our pizza and salad, my dad thanked each of my sisters and I for taking time from our hectic schedules to spend with him. Openly, he said he was sorry for being a selfish man when he was younger and not spending much time with us. He said that he wished things could have been different. He showed genuine remorse for not being the father we needed.

The next morning during breakfast with my four sisters, Raven unexpectedly made a confession to me. She spilled her true motives to exclude me. *"I coordinated and planned our visit to see dad in August. I didn't tell you because I didn't think you'd want to go,"* she admitted.

In a blink of an eye, it was time to say goodbye to our dad before us girls drove back home. Saying goodbye has never been easy for me. It floods me with rollercoaster emotions. Like each time I visited my dad as a child or teen and had to leave. I dreaded it.

The hardest part was knowing this time could very well be the last time I saw my father. He was in his eighties and not in good health. As my father and I hugged, saying goodbye, I told him how much I loved him. With tears in my eyes, I said it was great to see him and I would miss him.

Suddenly, I felt like that little girl standing in the airport getting ready to board the plane. I disliked leaving my father. I hated saying goodbye. There was a lump in my throat. Quietly, I told myself to be brave. To be grateful for the time we shared together.

Overall, the choice to reconcile with my dad has been the absolute best decision of my life. It's changed me. It's a special gift. It's healed me and my father wound. It fills me with peace.

After us five girls arrived home, we started unpacking our luggage out of Becky's car. Suddenly, I realized that my two pillows and other items were missing. I inquired, *"Has anyone seen my bag with my two pillows and eye mask?"*

Innocently, they echoed in unison, *"No, we haven't seen it."* This was very suspicious since they were the ones to pack our luggage inside of Becky's car. Earlier in the morning, I had felt dizzy and nauseous. My siblings claimed they took care of packing my belongings.

Before I left the hotel room, I examined the closet, bed, and room to double-check that they brought everything of mine. The room was empty. Therefore, I smelled a rat. Four sneaky rats who played mind-games and evil tricks on me.

Once inside the comfort of my home, I had no doubt in my mind who dumped my things behind my back. My pillows and items didn't randomly vanish out of thin air. It wasn't my vivid imagination, either. This was the beginning of the crazy-making flying monkeys who created stressful drama and chaos in my life.

SIX

Beware of Flying Monkeys

"In popular psychology, a flying monkey is someone who does the narcissist's bidding to inflict additional torment to the narcissist's victim. It might consist of spying on the victim, spreading gossip, threats, painting the narcissist as the victim, and their target as the perpetrator."

Author Unknown

If you have experienced narcissistic abuse, there's a likely chance you have encountered flying monkeys. Typically, they do the dirty work of the narcissist. According to Wikipedi.com, *"Flying monkey is a term mainly in the context of narcissistic abuse to describe people who act on behalf of the narcissist towards a third party, usually for an abusive purpose, such as smear campaigns."*

The term 'flying monkeys' is another way of saying 'abuse by proxy,' which is having someone else do the bidding for a narcissist. The term flying monkey was coined after the flying monkeys in the 1939 movie The Wizard of Oz. The flying monkeys were under the spell of the Wicked Witch of the East to do her bidding against Dorothy and her friends.

This common narcissistic tactic recruit's friends and family of the victim to spy on them. The flying monkeys will stalk the victim, gossip about them, spread rumors, retaliate, and start smear campaigns about them. All the while, they paint the narcissist as the victim. They accuse their target, the scapegoat, to be the culprit.

Flying monkeys can be your friends, co-workers, siblings, relatives, or the narcissist's friends, family, and/or co-workers. Flying monkey's stoop so low when they hunt for strangers to join their group of flying monkeys.

The narcissist is a master of manipulation. To maintain the illusion of power they have over you, a narcissist will employ the use of third parties to gaslight you, manipulate you, and bully you. They try to groom your friends, family, children, spouse, or intimate partner from the moment they meet them.

Initially, the narcissist is testing them. They want to see how strong your other relationship bonds are in effort to triangulate them. In the beginning, they may be charming towards your friends and family. Of course, this is to win their trust. They may tell them how much they love you or pay you dozens of complements. This test will determine if your friends and family go running back to you with this information.

On the surface, the narcissist and flying monkeys can appear sweet, caring, and kind. Behind the scenes, they're creating covert schemes to overpower your friends, family, and each of your relationships. They want to annihilate you!

Through time, the messages they feed your friends and family may begin to contain a small nugget of truth, except now the narcissist's poking fun at you behind your back. They may jokingly suggest, *"Susie is such a good storyteller. I never know if she's fibbing or not."*

This covert test is to plant a seed for later when you tell family and friends about the narcissists lies, manipulation, and bullying. The seed of doubt has now been carefully planted. Your friends and family may not believe what you say about the narcissist. Mission accomplished.

In an article on medium.com, titled, 'What's a Flying Monkey?' by Cherilyn Christen Clough, she shares two different types of flying monkeys. Clough states, "*There are two kinds of flying monkeys. Naïve flying monkeys are often children, elderly people or neighbors who have no clue what's going on. These naïve flying monkeys ask curious questions and are often set up by the narcissist to inquire for information or to say cutting things that might hurt the victim's feelings. The second group of flying monkeys is more toxic. They are often chosen by the narcissist because they already have angry or hate-filled personalities. If there was a case of sibling rivalry, the narcissist will choose the most bitter to attack the other. In this way, the narc parent can say they never said or did anything, while the victim is shamed, blamed and attacked by their sibling. This often leaves the victim feeling alone and scapegoated because they are obviously hated by their parent and sibling. The reality is they were both set up and pitted against each other in a cruel and hate-filled way while the narcissistic parent appears innocent. Despite which side they are on, and no matter how stupid or mean they appear, flying monkeys are always used by the narcissist. Flying monkeys are victims too in a way, but the most toxic flying monkeys don't care they were used because they justify the narcissist's unethical behavior. You might feel sorry for them, but in most cases, they get what they deserve — which is to become the scapegoat whenever the narcissist changes their mind. There's nothing stable or secure about the job of a flying monkey. It's a stooge's position.*"

17 Signs of Flying Monkeys

1. They gossip about you & spread terrible rumors.
2. They will spy on you via social media, the internet, & local functions.
3. Gaslighting & manipulation.
4. They will retaliate & aim to harm you.

5. They create smear campaigns against you, especially on social media.
6. They paint the narcissist as the poor victim & accuse you of being the abuser.
7. They stay loyal to the narcissist.
8. They defend & protect the narcissist.
9. Nonstop harassment by sending you offensive & cruel messages.
10. The flying monkeys will gang up on you. Oftentimes, they say, *"It's all of us and only you so the problem must be YOU!"*
11. Family mobbing, which is another way to gang up on you & hurt you.
12. The flying monkeys are control freaks. When they cannot control you, they will try to control how other people view you & what they think about you.
13. Flying monkeys will triangulate your relationships in effort to destroy them.
14. They will make false accusations about you secretly & in public. They enjoy trashing you & your credibility.
15. The flying monkeys are enablers for narcissistic abuse. They have a blind eye to all forms of abuse targeted at you, including physical, mental, sexual, financial, & spiritual abuse.
16. The flying monkeys practice the 3 D's: Denial. Deception. Dysfunction.
17. Some flying monkeys are extremely aggressive, domineering, & sociopathic.

Look Out for the Baiting Trap!

Baiting is the narcissist's deliberate act of provoking emotional reactions from you. It's to confirm their superiority and power over you. The madness and harm the pathological narcissist inflicts' onto you can keep you baffled for years. Narcissists are not the only one who use the covert baiting tactics. It is also what the flying monkeys do to you, including your relatives, bullies, and sociopaths.

For years, I was completely unaware of the term baiting. I didn't realize that my own mother, siblings, and strangers were purposely provoking me. During this time, I naively fell for it. In defense of myself, I fought back. I tried to justify myself. I made every effort to explain myself.

Good grief! This was precisely what they wanted from me. Their motive was for me to get upset, angry, and cry. To be stressed out. Unfortunately, in my younger years, I was extremely vulnerable.

In 2017, I woke up to what was going on. The dark veil departed. The fog lifted. Finally, I detected what my mom, sisters, and relatives tried to do to me. To get a negative emotional reaction from me. To turn my life upside down. To oppress and persecute me. To dump their toxic shame onto me.

Examples of Baiting: Practically every single time I visited my mom, she'd use her baiting maneuvers. No sooner would I arrive to her home when she'd say, *"You spoil your kids too much."* Oftentimes, she'd speak cruel about my children, husband, and myself. She'd provoke me by remarking on my appearance, accusing me of having large thighs or a big butt.

Instead of overreacting or fighting with her, I'd come back with a witty reply. I would laugh in her face, joking, *"Oh, men love it!"* Or I'd calmly respond, *"Actually, my legs and thighs are my best features."* The repulsive expression on her face was priceless. It ticked her off when I didn't fall for her BS!

When her tormenting words didn't work, she'd find other ways to manipulate me, gaslight me, and create conflicts with me. It was nonstop emotional chaos, drama, and lunacy.

Baiting is the act of deliberately annoying or provoking someone to extreme emotion. When a person intentionally baits another, they are deliberately taunting them in order to provoke a response from the offender's attack. Baiting, like fishing, is done to bully the scapegoat.

The narcissist targets you for fun. The scapegoat or black sheep in the family become the squirming worm on the hook.

Baiting is common on the internet, especially with cyberbullying, harassing, and stalking. The perpetrator will try to provoke you into a fight with them. They love tormenting you and watching you squirm! Due to their extreme insecurities about themselves, they puff themselves up by purposely criticizing you. People who have a sound mind would not behave that way.

I've experienced the baiting tactics on my YouTube channel and on social media. People with socially competitive personality types prone to tricking, manipulating, or deceiving others — especially for no other reason than to see if they can — are setting victims up for social abuse.

Tips to Not Take the Bait:

1. If you think someone is provoking you, don't react.
2. Remain calm. Take a slow deep breath to gain your composure.
3. Ignore the toxic person. This actually drives them nuts! They cannot stand being ignored because they desire to be the center of attention.
4. Baiting is a big part of the narcissistic supply. If you don't fall for it, they lose their power over you. They cannot control you. Then you are no longer fun. They become bored with you.
5. Baiting is a childish game. It requires at least two people; the toxic person & yourself. Do not play their mind games.
6. Don't engage with this person. Instead, end the conversation, & walk away.
7. Stand firm in your healthy boundaries. Consider going no contact with those malicious folks who insist on manipulating you.

14 Tips to Disarm Flying Monkeys & Narcissist

1. Acknowledge & be aware of your conscious reality.
2. Trust your gut instincts. If something feels off, good chance you are right.
3. On social media, your cellphone, & emails, block the flying monkeys & the narcissist.
4. If necessary, change your cellphone & landline numbers.
5. Do not engage with the narcissist & flying monkeys.
6. Set clear, healthy boundaries and maintain them.
7. Stop giving the narcissist & flying monkeys dozens of chances to redeem themselves. Accept that they are toxic & unhealthy.
8. Understand that you cannot fix, nor change the narcissist & flying monkeys.
9. Release all hope for reconciliation. In most cases, this is not realistic because they refuse to repent, they have no remorse, & they will never change.
10. In effort to start your healing journey, delete their pictures, text messages, and information off of your cellphone. Before you do this, take screenshots of potential evidence of their hostile threats & rude remarks.
11. Seek emotional support with a trustworthy friend or family member, licensed therapist, psychologist, or a Certified Trauma Recovery Coach.
12. If the flying monkeys or narcissist continue to contact you, bully you, or harass you, consider getting a restraining order. Seek legal counsel. Document all records of their negative comments, lies, threats, social media posts about you, retaliation, etc.
13. Consider going grey rock, which is limiting the amount of communication & time spent with toxic people. Less is best.
14. If your life, health, or safety is threatened, you may need to go full no contact. This means that you do not communicate in any way with the flying monkeys & the narcissist. You do not call them, text them, visit them, write letters to them. In

addition, you don't message them on or interact with them on social media. No contact means that you ended the abusive relationship.

Creating a long distance is ultimately the most effective strategy for permanently removing the narcissist and their flying monkeys from your life. This can be extremely tough and unpleasant, especially if they are family members or inextricably linked to your social life.

However, you must take care of yourself in every way possible. If it involves changing your name, packing your belongings, or moving to start a new life with a clean slate far away from the abusers, by all means do so.

SEVEN

Abusive Siblings: A Silent Epidemic

"Think about it — you cannot ask your sibling to move out. You are like a caged animal. You have to get along with people. So, with sibling abuse, there is a power imbalance. Someone is stronger or perceived to be stronger."

Laura Corbeth, Author of *My Courage to Tell: Facing a Childhood Bully and Reclaiming My Inner Child*

In 2018, I publicly disclosed that I had suffered toxic relationships with my sisters. Prior to uploading my first YouTube video on this sensitive topic, I had no idea if anyone else would relate. Shortly after this video went live, I received hundreds of comments by strangers who shared their stories of being bullied, manipulated, and abused by their own siblings. Three years later, these videos of mine now have over 35,620 views and thousands of comments.

Fast forward to October 2021 in which I've gained much more insight, wisdom, trauma-informed education, knowledge, and facts about the difference between sibling rivalry versus sibling abuse. There is a significant difference between the two. In this chapter, you will learn credible information pertaining to each of the traits and signs of sibling rivalry versus sibling abuse, plus recovery tips.

At this point in my healing journey, I have hundreds of videos about narcissists, flying monkeys, and a dysfunctional family. In addition, I have dozens of YouTube videos on various subjects pertaining to unhealthy relationships with brothers and sisters. I guarantee, if you have experienced it, you are not alone.

According to an article, Sibling Abuse and Bullying: The Hidden Epidemic on Psychology Today by Darlene Lancer, "*Often labeled rivalry and ignored, sibling bullying and abuse cause real trauma. Sibling abuse is the most common, but least reported abuse in the family. Prevalence is higher than spousal or child abuse combined with consequences well into adulthood similar to parent-child abuse. Up to 80% of youth experience some form of sibling maltreatment; yet it's been called the forgotten abuse.*"

Sibling abuse is underreported and goes under the radar. Typically, in early childhood, sibling rivalry can start out with squabbles, disagreements, name-calling, and competition between brothers and sisters. The rivalry is reciprocal. The motive is for parental attention. Moderate levels of sibling rivalry are a sign that each child is able to express his or her needs and wants.

Common Signs of Sibling Rivalry:

- Fighting
- Tattling
- Frustrations
- Being overdemanding
- Competing in school, sports, etc.
- Selfishness
- Teasing
- Name calling
- Constant bickering
- Jealousy
- Throwing temper tantrums

The concern with sibling rivalry is when it turns into sibling abuse. **The core root of sibling abuse is the intent to harm and control the other sibling**. Instead of it being a periodic incident, the abuse becomes a repeated pattern. This could carry on for months, years, and even decades.

It involves one or more siblings who takes the role of aggressor toward another who regularly feels disempowered. Sibling abuse includes ongoing bullying, harassment, and the motive to hurt the other sibling. Usually, an older child dominates a younger sibling who naturally tries to please his or her sibling.

Unlike rivalry, the intention is to establish superiority or to provoke fear and distress. Factors to consider include the motives, the degree of severity, a power of imbalance, victimization element, physical injuries, and trauma.

According to the website, Hope4Siblings.com, *"In America alone, there are over 40 million sibling abuse survivors. Society pays a huge price when sibling abuse is not given attention and goes uncorrected in lives of many adults. The over-learned maladaptive coping skills generated by an abusive sibling can affect adulthood. Because of sibling abuse, victimization occurred again in their childhoods through bullying. Sibling abuse is often directly connected to the formation of adult personality."*

Common Signs of Sibling Abuse:

- One sibling is extremely aggressive
- The other sibling feels helpless & powerless
- Imbalance of power
- Highly judgmental of the other sibling
- Tickle torture
- Bullying
- Gaslighting
- Controlling
- Intimidation
- Manipulative
- Cruelty
- Extreme envy
- Terrorizing the other sibling
- Pathological lying
- Degradation
- Scapegoating their sibling
- Retaliation after the other sibling sets boundaries
- Destroying the other sibling's possessions
- Physically abusing their sibling
- Spreading rumors about their sibling
- Smear campaigns against their sibling
- Ruining a sibling's reputation & career
- Emotionally abusing their sibling
- Sexually abusing their sibling
- Have friends gang up on their sibling
- Threats
- Sadistic behaviors to watch their sibling suffer
- Use of weapons

- Blame-shifting their sibling
- Recruiting other people to bully the sibling
- Stalking a sibling in person & online
- Withholding important information, including legal documents
- Stealing the family inheritance or trust fund from a sibling
- Excluding a sibling from attending their parent's funeral/memorial

Of the 34 common signs of sibling abuse listed up above, I've experienced 31 of them. Some occurred in my early childhood, but most took place during my adulthood, especially during the past three years. Obviously, this is a major reason why I chose to go no contact with my abusive sisters.

Neglectful Parents & Sibling Abuse

From early childhood through adulthood, parents often see an unhealthy dynamic between their kids, but they don't think much of it. They believe it's normal for siblings to push each other around, call each other names, and have conflicts. However, parents miss the point where it crosses the line to become psychological, mental, and sexual abuse.

Sibling abuse is evidence of a dysfunctional family unit. When we examine the generations before us, we can acknowledge that this is intergenerational trauma. Typically, in each generation, there is one parent and/or sibling who was the aggressor and one child and/or sibling who was the victim.

If one or both parents ignore the abused child's plea for help, it could cause the child a secondary trauma wound. Not only was the child tortured by their sibling, but their own parents denied that sibling abuse is real. For the traumatized child, they feel invalidated, dismissed, unheard, disbelieved, betrayed, and deeply hurt.

This toxic pattern within the broken family system will continue from one generation to the next, until one brave survivor finally ends the cycle of abuse. The dysfunction, bullying, and abuse didn't start with you, but it most certainly can end with you. I resonate with the quote by Stephi Wagner who wrote, *"Pain travels through families until someone is ready to feel it."*

Unfortunately, in some families the parents are unable to manage their own emotions to model appropriate behaviors. Due to emotionally immature parents and/or emotionally absent parents, they cannot be present for their children's feelings, challenges, and needs. Therefore, in some cases of sibling abuse, the parents give a blind eye to it. As heart-wrenching as this is, many trauma survivors have experienced this.

A big part of the problem is when the mother and father refuse to listen to their child. Despite their child disclosing sibling abuse, the parents ignore it, minimize it, or outright accuse the child of fabricating stories.

What this tells the child is that they're not important, they're too sensitive, they're just trying to get attention, and their own life has no value. Not only is this parental negligence devastating to the victim of sibling abuse, but it is quite traumatic. It can scar them for life.

Not all parents ignore the signs of sibling abuse. Some parents will quickly intervene on behalf of both children to seek professional help. The reality is that sibling abuse can occur in the best of homes and the worst of homes. However, there are some circumstances that could potentially lead to sibling rivalry that escalates to sibling abuse.

Examples of Sibling Abuse When Parent's Ignore Signs:

- Leave siblings together unsupervised
- Don't take an emotional interest in their children's lives

- Play favorites with the golden child
- Don't think there's anything wrong with their children fighting
- Haven't taught their children how to resolve conflicts in a healthy way
- Give more attention to one child over the other
- Neglects to stop their children's conflicts
- Scapegoats one of their children
- Deny that anything is wrong with their family dynamic
- Don't teach their children about personal boundaries

When the Abusive Bully Grows Up

What happens to the aggressive sibling who's the bully of the family? He or she may grow up to become a toxic adult bully. Oftentimes, they will harass other adults at college, work, on social media, in their community, and within their family of origin.

It's common that the role of the abusive sibling continues from childhood to adulthood. The only thing that changes is their age, their size, their physical strength, and how they choose to abuse their power. Instead of hairpulling as a child, they can become physically forceful towards other people; including with their adult sibling.

According to BullyingStatistics.org, *"One would think that as people mature and progress through life, they would stop behaviors of their youth. Unfortunately, this is not always the case. Sadly, adults can be bullies, just as children and teenagers can be bullies. While adults are more likely to use verbal bullying as opposed to physical bullying, the fact of the matter is that adult bullying exists. The goal of an adult bully is to gain power over another person, and make himself or herself the dominant adult. They try to humiliate victims and show them who is boss."*

The effects of sibling bullying and abuse mirror parent-child abuse. It can have a long-term negative impact on the survivors' sense of trust, safety, emotional health, physical health, and interpersonal relationships. The victims of sibling abuse of all ages may experience toxic shame, sadness, anger, low self-esteem, fear, depression, anxiety, guilt, and a lack of boundaries, especially if the abusive sibling and/or parents had accused the violated sibling of being 'the problem.'

According to Utterly Global, an organization dedicated to anti-bullying, *"Children who were bullies in grades six to nine are 60% more likely to have a criminal conviction by the age of 24. A bully is also five times more likely than a victim to have a serious criminal record in adulthood. Even bullies who grow up to work in an office instead of entering the judicial system cause problems for others."*

Adult Survivors of Sibling Abuse

Adult survivors of sibling abuse may continue to struggle with a wide range of negative symptoms and medical conditions, including Complex PTSD/PTSD, dissociation, triggers, flashbacks, nightmares, hypervigilance, and a fight, flight, freeze, or fawn response.

In addition, they may battle eating disorders, addictions, difficulty focusing, panic attacks, somatic complaints, fear of the dark, insomnia, autoimmune conditions, and/or chronic pain. Survivor trauma accumulates into compounded trauma and it's related to Adverse Childhood Experiences (ACEs), which is linked to codependency and negative health as adults.

Stages of Trauma Recovery Require the Survivor to:

1. Identify what took place
2. Name what happened (sibling abuse)
3. Name the perpetrators
4. Release 'traumatic amnesia,' which is living in denial, repressed memories, or not speaking the truth about your sibling abuse

5. Let go of guilt and toxic shame (It's not yours to carry)
6. Build awareness about sibling abuse & trauma
7. Educate yourself about all types of abuse; physical, mental, sexual, spiritual, and sibling abuse
8. Seek emotional support with a trauma-informed licensed therapist, psychologist, or Certified Trauma Recovery Coach who specializes in sibling abuse
9. If your sibling is currently abusive towards you or you feel unsafe, it is vital that you separate yourself from him or her

As an adult survivor of sibling abuse, the most difficult fact pertaining to it is that 90% of abusive siblings deny they have abused their sibling. They will not take accountability for it. Once I was able to grapple with this disturbing statistic, I chose to take the higher path towards healing.

My trauma recovery was not swift or easy. Rather, it has been an arduous trek. I've spent four years of processing what happened to me and addressing it. I understand that it wasn't my fault. I accept that my adult sisters and some of their family members are psychologically, physically, and/or sexually abusive.

I no longer permit myself to get tangled up in 'why me?' Instead, I actively choose to focus on the silver lining of what the negative experience has taught me. I am a big believer in finding the blessing in disguise.

I've learned that I am worthy of gentleness, respect, and decency. I have weeded out my old, limited beliefs about being a 'bad girl.' I have replaced it with positive affirmations, saying, *"I am a kindhearted, compassionate, empathic woman. I am divinely loved. People treat me with dignity, tenderness, and grace."*

While it may have taken me over five decades to learn valuable lessons, I now stand up for myself. I now believe in myself. I now trust my birthright is to love and to receive love. I now have confidence in myself and my life purpose. I now surround myself with respectful people who are trustworthy, authentic, and transparent souls who lift me higher. Most importantly, I am now filled with peace of mind, hope, and excitement for my future. I've come a long, long way!

EIGHT

Parental Triangulation & Alienation

"Parental Alienation is an emotional act of violence that is aimed at an adult, but critically wounds a child."

Steve Maraboli

When I was two years old, my parents divorced. Shortly after, my mother insisted we relocate far away from my father. It was such a long distance that it created long-term suffering and trauma for me; a painful father wound.

As a grown adult woman, I discovered in 2020 that I was a victim of parental alienation. Prior to this, I was not aware of the term 'parental alienation', nor what it meant. After educating myself to gain insight about it and after researching credible content online, I have now come to a new understanding of it.

My narcissistic mother had aggressively brainwashed me from my childhood through my adulthood. She tried to get me to think that my father didn't care about me, he didn't want to spend time with me, and he did not love me.

When an innocent child grows up to habitually hear this over and over, they start to believe it. They think it must be true. The child loves his/her mother and trusts them. The child is not emotionally mature to understand psychological abuse, triangulation of relationships, nor parental alienation.

This puts the child in the middle of their divorced parents, which can cause them to wrestle with who to be loyal to and who isn't trustworthy. I was indoctrinated to believe that my dad was a dishonest, selfish, horrible man. She convinced me that what she said was truthful. **No child should have to choose which parent to stay loyal to and which one to reject.**

Many survivors of narcissistic abuse understand triangulation of relationships. They clearly understand how the narcissist tried to destroy each of their relationships, including with their own children, spouse, siblings, parent, relatives, friends, co-workers, and partners.

What you may not have heard of or be aware of is that it's common for a narcissistic parent to alienate their children from the other parent. This is typical with a narcissistic parent who's divorced or separated to their spouse.

According to PsychologyToday.com, *"Parental alienation syndrome, a term coined in the 1980's by child psychiatrist Dr. Richard A. Gardner, occurs when one parent attempts to turn the couple's children against the other parent. A parent who is angry at the spouse or ex-spouse accomplishes this estrangement by painting a negative picture of the other parent via deprecating comments, blame, and false accusations shared with the children. They may 'hoard' the kids, doing all they can to thwart the other parent from spending time with them. In general, the alienating parent is the least emotionally healthy of the two."*

Parental alienation is a form of psychological abuse, which occurs when one parent removes the other parent from a child's life by way of brainwashing, gaslighting, and stonewalling the child. The perpetrator cleverly persuades the child to reject the other parent.

In most cases, especially with narcissistic abuse, a previously healthy and loving relationship between the child and their other parent is destroyed. This leads to severe emotional and psychological trauma to the child.

Who does parental alienation? It's most common by narcissistic parents and those who have borderline personality disorder. Due to how toxic and psychologically unstable they are, these types of people have no guilt or shame for intentionally alienating their children from the targeted parent.

How a Narcissist Alienates their Child with the Other Parent:

- Moving far away to create a long distance between the child and other parent
- Gossiping about the other parent and/or his new spouse
- Influencing the child to disrespect their other parent
- The narcissist is hostile, spiteful, and bitter towards the targeted parent
- Shift-blaming the other parent
- False accusations about the absent parent
- Limiting contact with the targeted parent
- The narcissist makes false allegations of abuse by the other parent
- Brainwashing the child to believe lies about the targeted parent
- Accusing the other parent of not caring for or loving the child
- Belittling and criticizing the absent parent
- Telling the child personal information about the marital relationship or reasons for the divorce, which is destructive for the child
- Forcing the child to choose one parent over the other
- The narcissist gets ticked off when the child spends time with their other parent and flies into an uncontrollable rage

- The narc parent uses the child to spy on & gather information about the targeted parent
- Making demands on the absent parent that is contrary to court orders
- Causing the child to become codependent with the narcissist

What is triangulation of relationships? On PsychCentral.com they shared, *"Triangulation is when a toxic or manipulative person, often a person with strong narcissistic traits, brings a third person into their relationship in order to remain in control. There will be limited or no communication between the two triangulated individuals except through the manipulator. It may appear in different forms, but all are about divide and conquer, or playing people against each other."*

Typically, the malignant narcissist will recruit flying monkeys to join them in their covert schemes to triangulate all of your relationships. They will triangulate your relationships with your siblings, other parent, relatives, friends, your own children, your spouse or partner, and your co-workers.

The narcissistic parent will constantly speak harshly, cruelly, and disrespectfully about the targeted parent. In addition, the narc will always play the victim card, blaming the absent parent for everything. Example: *"He cheated on me so he deserves to rot in hell."* Or *"I have no idea why your dad left me."* Once again, the toxic parent refuses to take ownership and accountability for their negative actions, words, and behaviors. They dump all blame onto the alienated parent.

A survey taken at the Association of Family and Conciliation Courts' annual (2014) conference reported 98% agreement *'in support of the basic tenet of parental alienation: children can be manipulated by one parent to reject the other parent who does not deserve to be rejected.'*

Here's a quote that nailed parental alienation on the head. *"If your ex wants to be involved with the life of a child you share and you keep them from doing so, you're not a badass parent and they are not a deadbeat.*

Parental alienation is real. It is a direct violation of their biological right to each other. Get the facts. Stop the abuse." (Author Unknown)

On the website, PsychologyToday.com, they shared, *"For the child, the biopsychosocial-spiritual effects of parental alienation are devastating. For both the alienated parent and child, the removal and denial of contact in the absence of neglect or abuse constitute cruel and unusual treatment...as a form of child maltreatment, parental alienation is a serious child protection matter as it undermines a basic principle of social justice for children: the right to know and be cared for by both of one's parents."*

Parental alienation involves the systematic brainwashing, manipulation, and lying to children with the sole purpose of destroying a loving and warm relationship they once shared with a parent. The most important fact to learn about parental alienation is that it is **child abuse.**

In 2017, after reading *The Father Effect* by John Finch, I felt nudged to visit my dad. It wasn't an easy choice, nor did it feel comfortable. Yet, I was compelled to make amends with him.

During our visit together, my father kept hugging me, smiling at me, and saying how happy he was to spend time with me. This was the beginning of our reconciliation. A powerful season to heal my father wounds.

It was a beautiful moment to understand that my dad has always loved me and cared about. Perhaps, he didn't know about parental alienation? Or maybe he realized that it was beyond his human control?

Despite what my mother had claimed about him not caring about me, I realized that my father most certainly did value me and his relationship with me. The one thing my narcissistic mother and toxic siblings cannot steal from me is that my father and I did restore our relationship. This has filled me with peace and it's a wonderful memory that I cling to, especially now that my father is deceased. In a later chapter, I will share details about my personal experience with my father wound and how my relationship was restored with my dad.

10 Signs You have a Trauma Bond

(AKA Stockholm Syndrome with a Narcissist)

What is a trauma bond? According to QuantumHealing.com, "*Trauma bonds are the toxic relationship between the abuser and the victim of the abusive relationship. It can be found in romantic relationships, between a child and abusive family members, or with a hostage and kidnapper situation.*"

A trauma bond is the type of emotional attachment that forms between abusers and victims, such as narcissistic parents and children or with a narcissistic partner. Trauma bonding can occur through the cycle of abusive behavior and positive behavior from the abuser. Through this way abusive behavior is normalized and whenever positive reinforcement is shown it can release an almost addictive-like dopamine rush, allowing for the abused person to disregard the negative behavior to only focus on the infrequent good behavior.

Let's take a look at Stockholm Syndrome, which is another name for traumatic bonding. According to Wikipedia.com, "*Stockholm syndrome is a condition in which hostages develop a psychological bond with their captors during captivity. Emotional bonds may be formed between captors and captives, during intimate time together, but these are generally considered irrational in light of the danger or risk endured by the victims.*"

Stockholm syndrome has never been included in the Diagnostic and Statistical Manual of Mental Disorders (DSM), the standard tool for diagnostic of psychiatric illnesses and disorders in the US, mainly due to the lack of a consistent body of academic research. There are four key components that characterize Stockholm syndrome:

1. A hostage's development of positive feelings towards the captor.
2. No previous relationship between hostage and captor.
3. A refusal by hostages to cooperate with police forces and other government authorities.
4. A hostage's belief in the humanity of the captor, ceasing to perceive them as a threat, when the victim holds the same values as the aggressor.

Stockholm syndrome is paradoxical because the sympathetic sentiments that captives feel towards their captors are the opposite of the fear and disdain which an onlooker might feel towards the captors. Stockholm syndrome describes the reactions of some abuse victims beyond the scope of kidnappings or hostage-taking. The most important fact to learn is that not all cases of trauma bonding entail a captor and captive dynamic.

Actions and attitudes similar to those suffering from Stockholm syndrome have also been found in victims of physical abuse, mental abuse, sexual abuse, child abuse, narcissistic abuse, human trafficking, and terrifying experiences.

10 Signs of Traumatic Bonding:

1. You walk on eggshells around the narcissist or abusive person.
2. You constantly worry that you will say or do something in which the narc will fly into an uncontrollable rage.
3. Despite how much the narcissist hurts you, you feel the need to protect them. Typically, this goes hand in hand with the narcissist brainwashing you to think they care about you.
4. When your friends, spouse, or relatives are disturbed by what the abuser is saying and doing to you, you defend the abuser. You may even take the blame or justify the despicable mistreatment.
5. Your relationship with the abusive person is not balanced, nor

mutual. It is very codependent, unhealthy, and quite toxic. The narcissist controls you and overpower you.

6. You are loyal to the abuser even though they haven't been loyal to you.
7. You are addicted to the narcissist. While you may not be aware of it, you are psychologically, physiologically, and biochemically addicted to your abuser. According to Katie Morten who's a licensed therapist, *"The rush of the stress hormone **cortisol**, and a flood of the feel-good chemical **dopamine** can trigger the reward center in our brain, which can cause you to think you're in love with your abuser."* (It's not love. It's a trauma bond.)
8. You justify or make excuses for the narcissist. *"He didn't mean to hit me. He was just upset."* Or *"She had a terrible childhood. I feel so sorry for her."*
9. You crave the crumbs of love and attention from the narcissist. Typically, the abuse alternates between moments of tenderness and turmoil. Perhaps, they gave you a gift, a complement, or claimed they loved you? Yet, any positive attention from the abuser is rare and infrequent compared to their nonstop manipulation, gaslighting, and cruel behaviors.
10. You feel trapped. Even after years of suffering abuse and trauma, you have stayed in this unhealthy, toxic relationship. You are scared to go no contact with the narcissist because you may fear for your safety. (Your safety will always come first. For some survivors, it's dangerous to leave.)

On the website, VeryWellMind.com, they stated that individuals with Stockholm Syndrome often report symptoms similar to PTSD. The symptoms may include:

- Being easily startled
- Distrust
- Feelings of unreality
- Flashbacks

- Triggers
- Inability to enjoy previously pleasurable experiences
- Irritability
- Nightmares
- Trouble concentrating
- Additional symptoms (dissimilar to PTSD) may include:
- Inability to engage in behavior that could assist in their release
- Negative feelings toward friends, family, or authorities who try to rescue them
- Positive feelings toward the captor
- Support of the captor's behavior (and the reasoning behind it)

Anyone can be susceptible to Stockholm syndrome. There are certain people with abusive backgrounds, including child abuse, domestic violence, sexual abuse, and narcissistic abuse that may be more likely to be affected. Any person can become a victim if the right conditions exist.

Understanding the underlying psychology surrounding a trauma bond and/or Stockholm syndrome can help you to manage the symptoms. Stockholm syndrome is the victim's response to trauma and involves many social dynamics. Some of these social dynamics include conformity, gaslighting, manipulation, romantic love, hoovering, stonewalling, and lack of education.

How to help yourself or other survivors of Stockholm Syndrome:

- **Psychoeducation** - This involves teaching victims about Stockholm syndrome and what it entails. Remember the saying, 'Knowledge is power?' Knowing what you're up against is the best offense to win the battle for yourself and/or your loved ones to break free from the toxic bonds with the narcissist.
- **Avoid Division** - Don't try to convince the victim of the

villainous traits of the abuser; this may cause the victim to polarize and defend the perpetrator. In my professional experience working with trauma survivors, not each person is ready or willing to admit, face, and accept that they have a trauma bond. Do not force this issue. It is not up for debates. Offer a listening ear, compassion, and empathy.

- **Use Curiosity** - Ask the victim good questions about how they see the situation, how they feel, what they think, and what they believe needs to happen next.
- **Listen Nonjudgmentally** - As the victim ponders everything that's happened and they process their experiences with the abuser, listen and use reflection to show genuine concern and validation.
- **Don't Give Advice** - Abuse survivors need to be empowered to make their own decisions. If you come along and tell them what to do because you 'obviously know better,' then you are not helping them to build personal power. Remember, the road to healing from abuse is often to empower the victim to make their own decisions, to know this, and to own it.
- **Address Cognitive Dissonance** - Being in a calculating relationship can cause cognitive dissonance, plus a wide range of normal trauma responses, such as dissociation. In some cases, the survivor's intuition isn't functioning. They doubt their own selves. They may not trust themselves or their gut instincts. They may be confused about their own conscious reality. Help them by validating their truth and encouraging them to trust themselves.
- **Identify the 'hook'** - Victims of Stockholm syndrome can become dedicated to a cause or an unspoken desire. They may over-identify with the predator in a dysfunctional, codependent way in order to fulfill a personal need. This is the 'hook.' Help the victim identify what the underlying need is that is being fulfilled by the abusive relationship connection. Once a victim understands why they are so

committed to the relationship, they can start making positive improvements to focus on their own lives.

Some examples of hooks include feeling the need to be devoted, dedicated, and loyal to the narcissist. This can be found in statements, such as *"I'll be there no matter what,"* or *"It's you and me against the world."* These types of needs tend to be unconscious and may have developed at an earlier stage of an individual's younger life.

Being aware of the psychological underpinnings of trauma bonding can help you understand how to best help yourself and/or someone with the condition. Ultimately, no matter what intervention you use to help someone who has Stockholm syndrome, remember to offer empathy, sensitivity, and grace.

NINE

Narcissistic Abuse, Complex PTSD, & Chronic Pain

"Narcissistic parents cause enormous harm to their children. When grown, these victims of narcissistic abuse face seemingly insurmountable problems, including the formation of complex post-traumatic stress disorder."

The CPTSD Foundation

Abuse can take many forms, from physical violence to coercive control. Narcissistic abuse is something that often gets overlooked. It's a very subtle form of psychological abuse. Many people have suffered PTSD, Complex PTSD, and/or chronic pain from narcissistic abuse. It's something that can occur in relationships, including marriages, friendships, families, and partnerships. It can have a lasting, devastating impact on survivors.

In effort to build awareness about the link between abuse, Complex PTSD, and chronic pain, I am going to share my experiences. In March 2008, I was diagnosed with primary fibromyalgia. Not just once, but it was confirmed twice by two different specialists. Most medical testing for autoimmune disorders can be hit or miss. In some cases, traditional doctors can miss early childhood neglect, abuse, sexual assaults, domestic violence, and narcissistic abuse. Undiagnosed trauma is the missing link.

Ironically, not a single doctor, therapist, nor psychiatrist asked me if I had ever suffered child neglect, abuse, sexual assaults, domestic violence, or narcissistic abuse. No one ever inquired if I suffered trauma. For five decades, I missed the common thread between verbal abuse, physical abuse, sexual abuse, a dysfunctional family, and the direct connection with trauma.

The million-dollar question: Why is the medical and the mental health industry not asking patients these important questions? How come countless abuse survivors fall through the cracks and they don't receive appropriate care? Why do doctors dish out potent prescriptions as if it were candy? Why are some professionals not trained about abuse? How come they are unaware of the subtle signs? Most importantly, why are they not educated or trauma-informed?

In Western medicine and the mental health community, doctors, therapists, and psychiatrists are trained to hyper-focus on the patient's symptoms. They are trained to treat the symptoms with medicine. Yet, they don't get to the **root** cause.

Not only do they overlook the root cause, but they refuse to consider natural solutions. They neglect to view patients as a whole human being; body, mind, and soul. We are not just a physical person. We are a whole human being with emotions and a soul. Unfortunately, some of us survivors have deep trauma wounds that continue to bleed.

Over the past 13 years, my healing journey with fibromyalgia, CPTSD, and compounded trauma has had many bumps in the road. Ups and downs, which led me to look outside traditional medicine. These desperate moments prompted me to rescue my own self. To learn how to recover holistically and gently.

Here's a few vital facts I've learned the hard way. Cymbalta didn't help me. It hurt me. Benzodiazepines were a horrifying nightmare with wicked withdrawals. They took my life, health, dreams, relationships, my mind, ability to parent my children, and my career hostage. It disabled me and traumatized for me. It was a wake up call for me to educate myself about prescriptions, side effects, and the horrifying long-term implications.

Medicine, such as antidepressants and anti-anxiety drugs, can cause patients to numb out. To dull their pain. Patients may experience memory loss, brain fog, cognitive impairment, forgetfulness, lack of concentration and focus, and the inability to feel their emotions. In addition, patients may become emotionally detached, withdrawn, and completely unaware of their conscious reality in the present moment. It's common for patients to have 'flatlined emotions.' Therefore, survivors cannot heal their trauma because they cannot feel their human emotions.

While there is a time and a place for traditional medicine, it should not be the first or only option. It can be temporarily helpful, but not beneficial for long-term treatment. We must understand that long-term use of psychotropic prescriptions can negatively harm the central nervous system, neurotransmitters, the brain, and the organs in the body. Prescriptions can sabotage the recovery process for trauma patients.

Add fragmented memories, dissociation, triggers, flashbacks, and a disconnection from themselves, plus a flood of trauma responses, which complicate the circumstances. Most trauma survivors cannot recall every detail about their hellish ordeal. Our bodies want to protect us. It is common for survivors to dissociate and to not recall all of the details involved with their traumatic event.

Dissociation is linked to abuse and trauma; one-time events and long-term experiences. It is a coping strategy the brain uses to manage severe trauma and life after the initial traumatic event. Dissociation is a mental process where a person disconnects from their mind, thoughts, feelings, memories, and their sense of identity.

During trauma, some people may have an 'out of body' experience. This is our body and brain trying to protect us from danger. We automatically go into survivor mode. Oftentimes, our bodies and minds are on high alert. Even after the abuse or trauma ended. We may find ourselves battling fight, flight, freeze, or fawn. Even if we hope to forget about our traumatic experiences, our body and brain will never forget it. Our body and brain will remember. It can show up as triggers, nightmares, flashbacks, anxiety, insomnia, physical pain, and feeling unsafe.

In retrospect, I never needed medicine. Not Effexor, Prozac, Cymbalta, Adderall, nor Ativan. I most certainly didn't need mind-warping prescriptions. The root of my condition wasn't anxiety, depression, nor mental instability. **The root was compounded trauma and Complex PTSD.**

My compounded trauma contained layers upon layers of years suffering neglect and abuse. Child neglect and abuse. Multiple sexual assaults. Growing up in a dysfunctional family. Being a daughter of a narcissistic mother. Plus, experiencing habitual psychological abuse, bullying, gaslighting, manipulation, stalking, and smear campaigns by my mom, sisters, and their families. It took me over fifty years to receive an accurate diagnosis for my compounded trauma and Complex PTSD. It's ludicrous that it took this long.

The statistics linking fibromyalgia and trauma are shocking. According to the Institute of Chronic Pain, *"Upwards of 90% of women with fibromyalgia syndrome report trauma in either their childhood or adulthood and 60% of those with arthritis report such a trauma history."*

One study looked at 385 people over the age of 60 years old who were diagnosed with fibromyalgia. The results speak loud and clear:

- Over 70% of women and 67% of men had experienced trauma.
- Over 50% of women and 60% of men experienced neglect and abuse.
- Over 54% of people had experienced physical abuse.

- Almost 50% of women had experienced sexual assault.

Following abuse and trauma, the body can manifest physical and emotional pain. It can show up years later after the first trauma occurred. My own physical pain and troubling symptoms appeared at least seven years before my official fibromyalgia diagnosis. During that time, I was only 37 years old.

My symptoms included fatigue, excruciating migraines, muscle weakness, chronic fatigue, chronic sore throat, countless allergies with food and seasonal allergies, extreme sensitivity to medicine, brain fog, memory loss, lack of focus, cognitive impairment, severe insomnia, GI distress, chronic kidney stones, muscular pain, constipation, urinary conditions, UTI's, backpain, herniated disks, joint stiffness, thyroid conditions, triggers, flashbacks, depression, anxiety, and debilitating physical pain throughout my entire body. These symptoms hindered my ability to function and to work on a daily basis.

In those earlier days, I never connected the dots to my abuse and trauma. I was unaware that my ongoing physical and emotional challenges were linked to my trauma. It wasn't until 2017, a decade later, when I clearly understood the correlation between fibromyalgia and trauma.

My memoir, *Soul Cry: Releasing & Healing the Wounds of Trauma*, shares how the #MeToo movement helped to shine the light on such a dark experience. Here's an excerpt from *Soul Cry*: *"In 2017, after the Hollywood producer, Harvey Weinstein's sexual assault scandal went viral, the #MeToo movement grew like wildfire. It triggered my sexual trauma. Painful flashbacks. Triggers. My increased anxiety and intense insomnia wrecked me. Old memories resurfaced with a vengeance. A floodgate of horrific injustices knocked me off of my feet. Like when I had been a little girl and my babysitter abused me. When I was 15 years old and a party turned into statutory rape. When I suffered sexual assault in mid-life by my sister's husband. When I endured a lifetime of abuse by my malicious mother.*

The atrocious incidents were reminders that I still hadn't recovered. Each was a nightmare. A horror which I didn't want to relive. Layer upon layer of my deep wounds stung badly. Feeling betrayed, I questioned who I could trust. I lost all faith and confidence in my mom and siblings. They treated me worse than my enemies. The illusion of my 'happy family' became dismantled. Sexual trauma is quite complex and individualized. The magnitude of my trauma felt paralyzing. For many years, I couldn't face it. The severity was a massive weight for me to process. I felt powerless to help my own self. Part of me wanted to erase the nightmare from my mind. Yet, it kept cropping up out of nowhere. Unconsciously, I dissociated from my abuse and trauma. Mentally, I withdrew and detached from the situation. I buried my horrible memories. I tried everything within my ability to drown out the voices screaming for help."

Dear friend, I hear your soul cry. I know firsthand the toxic shame and pain of abuse, including with a narcissist. Perhaps, you are still wrestling with your past trauma? Or you were silenced by those who betrayed you and hurt you?

Bessel A. van der Kolk, who is an author, trauma educator, author, and psychiatrist brings' wisdom, understanding, and insight into how trauma impacts the body, mind, and brain. He is the bestselling author of the book, *The Body Keeps the Score: Brain, Mind, and Body in the Healing of Trauma.* He wrote, *"The trauma caused by childhood neglect, sexual or domestic abuse, and war wreaks havoc on our bodies. Traumatized people chronically feel unsafe inside their bodies: The past is alive in the form of gnawing interior discomfort. Their bodies are constantly bombarded by visceral warning signs, and in an attempt to control these processes, they often become expert at ignoring their gut feelings and in numbing awareness of what is played out inside. They learn to hide from themselves."*

One concern for the chronic pain community is when they rarely address the connection to trauma. The average person doesn't realize how past abuse and trauma can later manifest itself into full blown medical conditions, such as fibromyalgia. Instead of considering the root cause, they mainly focus on symptoms, prescriptions, and invasive procedures, which can directly lead to secondary symptoms and further complications. It is unfortunate that this can turn into a vicious cycle. Perhaps, it's time to jump off the medical merry go round?

Unresolved abuse and trauma can hinder the healing pathway. Denial is a maladaptive coping mechanism, which is unhealthy. It keeps the patient stuck. We must learn that if we ignore, minimize, or bury our trauma, it will continue to haunt us. It is a form of self-sabotage.

We must not pretend that our abuse didn't happen. Even if the perpetrator was your sibling, mom, dad, spouse, clergy, or intimate partner. We must not try to 'move on' or 'just get over it' without facing it. If you bury your pain, how can you resolve the core issues of your trauma? Running or numbing from your pain is not the least bit helpful. It will keep you going in circles and amplify your agony.

It makes more logical sense to unravel the root of the problem. To resolve the core concerns. To have the courage to dig into the depth of your soul to acknowledge your trauma, address it, and confront what is hurting you. Dr. Gabor Mate', who's a bestselling author, speaker, physician, and trauma expert, stated, *"The attempt to escape from pain is what creates more pain."*

If you are still hurting from past abuse, I ask you to consider talking to at least one trustworthy person. It can be a close friend, family member, trauma-informed therapist, psychologist, or a Certified Trauma Recovery Coach. Another therapeutic method is to journal. To write where it hurts in a vulnerable way. To write what upsets you, disturbs you, angers you, grieves you, and what has traumatized you. To let the tears flow. To write truthfully and honestly about those who have deeply harmed you, including the narcissist and/or other perpetrators.

It takes great courage and strength to acknowledge, confront, and process your trauma. To admit to yourself, *"Yes, it did happen. Yes, it really was that bad."*

It has been two decades of ongoing challenges in my health. I have fought for my life. I have battled for my body, mind, future, and trauma recovery. If there is nothing else that I have learned about myself when it comes to the toll of trauma, it is this: **I am a courageous survivor.**

Despite my fibromyalgia, back pain, compounded trauma, and Complex PTSD, I have empowered myself to regain 80% of my health. Was it hard? Absolutely! It was an atrocious ordeal for me. Yet, no matter how dreadful it's been, I am worth fighting for. My healing is worth fighting for. My life matters and so does yours.

Another amazing revelation is coming to see that I have been transformed. I've experienced a beautiful metamorphosis similar to the butterfly. I have grown as a human being, gained wisdom about pharmaceutical drugs, and I have learned credible information about a holistic approach. In addition, I have educated myself about trauma, how to heal my trauma, and how to help other survivors to heal their trauma. I have found practical tools to heal naturally, gently, and safely.

Even more exciting, I have found my voice, especially on my YouTube channel and in my books. I am flourishing! This had led to my becoming the voice to the voiceless. To give hope to the hopeless. To advocate and educate on behalf of others who are survivors of child abuse, sexual abuse, domestic violence, CPTSD, trauma, narcissistic abuse, and sibling abuse.

Tips for the Trauma Recovery:

- **Become a Truth Seeker** – Be honest with yourself about your past abuse, sexual assaults, grief, loss, betrayal, and negative experiences. Be brave and speak your truth.
- **Don't Bury Your Pain** – Avoid blocking your pain, burying your pain, and numbing from your traumatic events.
- **Feel It to Heal It** – Give yourself permission to feel your authentic emotions; positive and negative. Allow yourself to tap into your feelings that rise to the surface of your conscious reality. It is okay to not feel okay about your emotions. It's helpful to observe our emotions and memories without judging them. When we give ourselves time to feel and express our painful emotions, we can process and move through them to heal them.
- **Grief & Loss** – Learn and understand the five stages of grief. They are denial, bargaining, anger, depression, and acceptance. It is common for trauma survivors to feel outraged and upset about their past abuse. You were violated! You were mistreated, betrayed, and victimized. You have every right to feel however you may feel. Find productive and healthy ways to express your anger, sadness, frustration, and grief. Exercise to boost your 'feel good endorphins.' Punch a pillow. Visit a 'rage room,' which is a safe business to let loose by throwing plates, glasses, and objects to release your anger. It's okay to scream, cuss, vent, and cry. Another idea is to go into the woods where you are alone and yell as loud as you want. It actually feels good to get this heavy burden off of your shoulders. Keep in mind that all forms of abuse and trauma are a loss. You may have lost your parent, sibling, spouse, intimate partner, or a friend, especially if they are the covert narcissist, flying monkeys, or the perpetrator. Or in my case, you lost your entire family of origin. Yes, it does hurt. It is a significant loss. Moving through grief is essential in your

recovery journey. There is no timeline for grief. Grief is like the ocean. It ebbs and it flows. There can be moments when you feel as if you are being tugged under fierce waves of grief. You may feel like you are drowning in a river of tears. Other times, you may appear to be afloat and doing alright. It's normal to bounce from one stage of grief to the next. Or to get stuck in one stage of grief, such as anger. Grieve for as long as it takes to fully express it, process, and to release your legitimate sorrow and pain.

- **Avoid Self-Medicating & Alcohol** - Addictions are linked to trauma. It's common for abuse survivors to self-medicate and use alcohol, or other types of addictions to 'dull the pain.' However, this maladaptive coping mechanism only causes more harm and heartbreak. It can cause destructive patterns in an unhealthy coping method. Addiction and trauma expert, Gabor Mate' has shared educational speeches and YouTube videos on this important topic. He shared, *"Not all addictions are rooted in abuse or trauma, but I do believe they can all be traced to painful experience. A hurt is at the center of all addictive behaviors. It is present in the gambler, the Internet addict, the compulsive shopper and the workaholic. The wound may not be as deep and the ache not as excruciating, and it may even be entirely hidden—but it's there. As we'll see, the effects of early stress or adverse experiences directly shape both the psychology and the neurobiology of addiction in the brain."* (Excerpt is from his book, *In the Realm of Hungry Ghosts: Close Encounters with Addiction*)
- **Forgive Yourself** – If you're reading this book, it's likely that you have experienced abuse and trauma. Or your loved one has suffered abuse. Some survivors may feel upset with themselves for their traumatic event. When you were much younger, you didn't know what you did not know. Give yourself forgiveness and grace. You are not responsible for the perpetrators and abusers. Please know that your abuse was **never** your fault.
- **Self-care** – Offer yourself and your inner child tenderness,

kindness, and nurturing. On a daily basis, try to do at least one nice thing for yourself. A few examples include, watching your favorite comedy show, soak in a warm Epsom salt bath, read your favorite book, treat yourself to a beautiful bouquet of flowers, watch sports, enjoy your hobby, or spend time in nature.

- **Seek Emotional Support** – If you have experienced child neglect, abuse, bullying, narcissistic abuse, mental abuse, sexual abuse, domestic violence, trauma, or betrayal, please reach out to a trauma-informed specialist who's educated and knowledgeable about the specific type of trauma you've experienced. It may be a counselor, clergy, psychologist, close friend, spouse, online support group, or a Certified Trauma Recovery Coach. You do not need to be a lone ranger and isolate yourself. Instead, connect with trustworthy, likeminded people and/or professionals who offer you compassion, validation, and empathy in a safe environment.
- **Educate Yourself** – Be open to learn something new. Be willing to step outside your comfort zone to read, learn, and gain knowledge about narcissistic abuse, toxic relationships, sexual assault, mental health, chronic pain, and trauma. There are dozens upon dozens of gentle, natural ways to decrease depression, anxiety, panic attacks, insomnia, chronic pain, migraines, autoimmune disorders, and medical conditions. In addition, there are many effective methods for helping trauma survivors to move through their memories and pain in a safe environment. A few examples are bodywork, Somatic Experiencing, Emotional Freedom Technique, massage therapy, EMDR, art therapy, energy work, and acupuncture.

Child abuse, narcissistic abuse, bullying, gaslighting, toxic siblings, physical abuse, mental abuse, sexual assaults, domestic violence, and dysfunctional families are directly linked to trauma. Dr. Peter Levine sums up trauma perfectly. He said, *"Trauma is perhaps the MOST avoided, ignored, belittled, denied, misunderstood, and untreated cause of human suffering."*

Regardless of a lack of emotional support, education, training, and/or understanding about trauma, **all survivors deserve to heal.** Each survivor deserves to be heard. To be seen. To be believed. To be validated. To be treated with dignity, empathy, and respect.

We each have a story. May *Soul Rescue* inspire you to raise your own voice. To not permit others to silence or shame you. To stand up for yourself. To do what you believe is right. To create boundaries. To become proactive in your own personal healing.

No matter what you are struggling with today, have hope for your trauma recovery. Learn to advocate for yourself. Seek credible education about trauma, chronic pain, and CPTSD. It can empower you. It may be the healing balm to set you onto the right path for your recovery. You are worthy of healing. I am cheering you on!

TEN

Healing Toxic Shame

"Our need to be 'greater than' or 'less than' has been a defense against toxic shame. A shameful act was committed upon us. The perpetrator walked away, leaving us with the shame. We absorbed the notion that we are somehow defective. To cover for this, we constructed a false self, a masked self. And it is this self that is the overachiever or the dunce, the tramp or the puritan, the powermonger or the pathetic loser."

Maureen Brady, *Beyond Survival: A Writing Journey for Healing Childhood Sexual Abuse*

Toxic shame is a serious concern for those who have survived narcissistic abuse. This type of shame goes far beyond thinking, *"I made a big mistake"* or *"I regret doing something."* Toxic shame is usually dumped onto people by their toxic family, spouse, intimate partner, or ex. It's done in a very subtle, sneaky way.

Toxic shame can have you believing, *"I'm a bad person because I did ________."* Fill in the blank. You could feel toxic shame because you ended a destructive relationship. You may feel toxic shame because your sibling sexually assaulted you. You can struggle with toxic shame if you have a low self-worth. You may experience toxic shame if you're still in the midst of processing your trauma.

In other words, toxic shame judges the person (yourself), rather than the act of what someone inflicted upon you; psychological abuse and trauma. Oftentimes, survivors are not consciously aware if they have toxic shame. They may have grown up with it. In addition, it could be hidden and buried deep within your subconscious mind.

When shame becomes toxic, it can eat at us and destroy our lives. Everyone experiences shame on occasion. It's an emotion with physical symptoms like any other that comes and goes. When it's severe, it can cause extreme pain. You may battle strong feelings of shame, which stimulate your nervous system, causing you a fight-flight-freeze trauma reaction. You can feel exposed. You may want to run away, hide, or react in anger. You may feel overwhelmed by confusion or not be able to think clearly.

Worse, you may feel intensely alienated from others and the good parts of yourself. This is common if you are no longer in contact with the narcissist and other perpetrators. You can be consumed with self-contempt, which is escalated since you're unable to be rid of yourself. You can experience triggers or tender spots that produce feelings of shame. The intensity of your experience varies, too, depending upon your prior life experiences, cultural beliefs, personality, and your traumatic events.

Toxic Shame Traits:

- **Isolation** – With unhealthy shame, you may isolate yourself for a long time. Your friends and family may try to coax you to come out of your shell. You may isolate because you are suffering toxic shame, fear, and an overall sense of being unsafe.
- **False Masks** – If you have toxic shame, one common sign is that you will not feel comfortable being yourself. You may

cover up your true identity. The shame of this nature can cause you to feel like you're not accepted by society, friends, and family. Therefore, you may subconsciously create a 'more appealing' version of yourself to look better by others.

- **Mental Health** – Those who are dealing with toxic shame may spiral out of control. They may battle depression, anxiety, CPTSD, despair, and hopelessness.
- **Silenced** – Whatever happened to cause your shame, you stay silent about it. You may refuse to speak up about your abuse. Your toxic shame is intensified to such a high degree that you feel paralyzed to disclose the truth.
- **Denial** – Due to how traumatic toxic shame can become, you may live in denial about your past abuse. You may have a very difficult time admitting and talking about what happened to you. It may hurt so deeply that you are stuck in a denial stage.
- **Disturbing Memories** – You may have nightmares, flashbacks, and horrible memories that show up in your sleep, in images during a waking state, or in your negative beliefs that originated in your childhood. It can be linked to your 'shame story' about your abuse, trauma, and violent acts that were done to you.
- **Shame-based Beliefs** – Toxic shame creates a sense of being inadequate. You may feel unlovable, unworthy, defective, not good enough, like a fraud, and/or not important.

In most cases, shame becomes internalized from chronic experiences of shame that were dumped onto you in your childhood. Parents, especially narcissistic, can transfer their shame to their children through verbal words and nonverbal behaviors. For example, a child may feel unlovable in reaction to their parent's neglect, abuse, absence, and/or indifference. If not resolved, toxic shame can lead to depression, anxiety, PTSD, CPTSD, addictions, eating disorders, aggression, low self-esteem, irrational guilt, perfectionism, codependency, and/or unhealthy relationships as an adult.

How can we heal toxic shame? If you've fallen victim to toxic shame, there is still hope for a full recovery. Despite it originating from childhood trauma, you can still learn to conquer this self-defeating behavior.

> *"Shame is internalized when one is abandoned. Abandonment is the precise term to describe how one loses one's authentic self and ceases to exist psychologically."*
>
> John Bradshaw, Author of *Healing the Shame that Binds You*

Since toxic shame is internalized and it's linked to abandonment, you can start to shift your subconscious mind by first reconnecting to your inner child and your adult self.

Being compassionate with yourself is one of the most important things to do in order to let go of unhealthy emotions. Keep in mind, we are all human and imperfect. You don't need to be perfect. You are enough just as you are today. Many of us are healing from something that victimized us or traumatized us.

Dear friend, please be gentle with yourself. It's okay to cut yourself a little slack. The active way to start doing this is by using positive words, thoughts, beliefs, and affirmations about yourself. Each day, say things like, *"I am worthy," "I am unconditionally loved,"* and *"My life has value and incredible importance."*

Healing begins within. The ability to heal starts in your subconscious mind. If you think you cannot recover, you won't. If you believe that you will recover, you will. The subconscious mind is extremely powerful. What you feed it, positive or negative, is exactly the results you will get.

Therefore, pay attention to your thoughts, words, and beliefs. Build awareness about it because it correlates to your conscious reality. In addition, pay attention to the people, places, and things that you interact with; face to face and online. What are you feeding your mind? Is it healthy and boosting your overall attitude or is it poisonous and destroying your life?

Interesting facts about the subconscious mind: (Found on https://themindsjournal.com)

- It records everything.
- It's always alert and awake.
- It controls 95% of our lives.
- It is built on habituation.
- It speaks to you in dreams.
- It has no verbal language.
- It can do trillion things at once.
- It is not logical; it's the feeling mind.
- It's one million times powerful than the conscious mind.

Mindfulness, through things like meditation, prayer, journaling, and daily affirmations, reminds us about the truth. It helps us to stay in our present moment. It's empowering to connect to likeminded people who have a similar practice of speaking love, peace, unity, harmony, healing, and encouragement into our own lives.

It can shift your energy and help you build momentum in your healing journey. Through time, consistency, and practice, taking your thoughts and words captive can help you realize how strong you truly are and how you can get through anything, including past abuse.

Also, you can learn to turn that inner voice of toxic shame into empathy towards yourself. Give yourself the love, warmth, and nurturing that you didn't receive as a child. Have the courage to let yourself be seen. Let yourself be heard. Tap into your authentic emotions. No matter what you feel, your emotions are valid. It's time to kick toxic shame to the curb!

According to Laura Giles, LCSW, *"Shame comes from invalidation. Healing comes from validation. Something magical happens when you tell your story and you're believed. Your experience is real. Your feelings are valid. You are important. Shame thrives in isolation. Healing comes from connecting. It may feel counterintuitive to be vulnerable when that's exactly what got you hurt. That's precisely what healing asks of you. Let yourself shine little by little in authentic ways until it becomes the new norm. You can break this pattern and thrive.*

Warning Signs You're in Abusive Relationships

Are you currently involved with one or more abusive relationships? If so, this psychoeducational content can help you to learn the warning signs of harmful relationships and offer you helpful tips to end the abuse cycle.

According to StopRelationshipAbuse.org, *"Relationship abuse is a pattern of abusive and coercive behaviors used to maintain power and control over a person. Abuse can be emotional, financial, sexual, or physical. It can include threats, isolation, and intimidation."*

Who are the perpetrators? They can be your:

1. Father or mother
2. Brothers or sisters
3. Other relatives
4. Intimate partner
5. Spouse
6. Ex-partner or ex-spouse
7. Friend
8. Co-worker
9. Manager or supervisor
10. Roommate

Typically, the manipulation, gaslighting, and abuse tends to escalate over time. When someone has abusive or violent behaviors, it's perpetual toxic patterns of control. Physical assault is easier to recognize; bruises, cuts, scars, or broken bones. Whereas, mental abuse, bullying, and sexual abuse can be more insidious. Oftentimes, it goes undetected by the victims, their family members, and friends.

Mental Abuse to Gain Power & Control, may include:

1. Insults
2. Harsh judgements
3. Name-calling
4. Criticisms
5. Gaslighting
6. Swearing
7. Ridiculing
8. Stonewalling
9. Manipulation
10. Bullying & stalking
11. Deceit & denial
12. Threats
13. Lying, stealing, or cheating

15 Warning Signs You're in Abusive Relationships:

1. After habitually hurting you, the toxic person has 'selective amnesia.' Suddenly, they claim, *"I don't know what you're talking about."* Or *"I cannot remember."*
2. They accuse you of doing & saying things that you didn't do or say. This is a clear sign of projection.
3. They are highly manipulative & sneaky.
4. The abuser will gaslight you & make you doubt your own sanity.
5. They will try to make you feel guilty or ashamed in effort to blame-shift you.
6. They're pathological liars & constantly cover up the truth.
7. They lack empathy and remorse for abusing you.

8. They accuse you of being the crazy one!
9. Typically, they have a Jekyll & Hyde persona. One minute they're super sweet to you, but the next minute they're cussing you out.
10. They have abrupt mood changes & emotional dysregulation. You walk on eggshells.
11. During an argument, they use physical force to hurt you.
12. They have extreme jealousy of you, your other relationships, including with your friends, family, pets, your children, & anything positive happening in your life.
13. The toxic person is very controlling of you, your life, your health, your job, your appearance, what you wear, etc.
14. They punish you for setting healthy boundaries. They continue to disrespect you & your boundaries.
15. They play the 'victim card.' If anything goes wrong, they say it's your fault. Oftentimes, they accuse you of being the offender when it's THEM.

All forms of relationship abuse are extremely traumatic and painful. Please know that if someone has abused you in the past or currently abusing you, it is **not** your fault.

Common Emotions that are a Normal Trauma Response:

- Confused
- Exhausted
- Emotionally & physically drained
- Sadness
- Anger
- Grief & loss
- Trapped
- Heartbroken
- Betrayed
- Helpless & powerless

- Depression & anxiety
- Toxic shame & guilt

Despite the lame excuses of why someone hurt you, relationship abuse is not caused by alcohol, drugs, stress, anger management, or provocation. YOU DIDN'T DO ANYTHING WRONG. Ultimately, it is the perpetrator's choice to be abusive. **We must hold the abusers accountable.** It sends a clear message to others that abuse will not be tolerated.

Options to End the Abuse Cycle:

- Seek emotional support with a licensed therapist, psychologist, or Certified Trauma Recovery Coach.
- Speak to at least one trustworthy person.
- Go no contact with abusive people, including family members.
- Contact your local authorities and/or an attorney.
- Get a restraining order if you feel unsafe or if someone threatens you.
- Document what they say and do. One never knows if they will land in court. The documents are your evidence that yes, the abuse did happen. And yes, it really was that bad.
- Call the National Domestic Violence hotline at 1-800-799-7233.

You cannot heal in the same toxic environment and abusive relationships, which deeply hurt you. Healing requires you to name the abusers. To acknowledge it. To address it. To face what they did and said to you. To love yourself enough that you bravely reclaim your life to rescue your own self.

ELEVEN

How to Break Free from Narcissistic Abuse

"You are going to detox. No contact is your rehab center. This will bring you back to life and heal you. It will detox you of all the toxicity of the dysfunctional family. It's like a cleansing fire. You have to feel the heartbreak, the loss, and let it go. No contact is a powerful tool on the road to healing from narcissistic abuse. Big changes like this are often very painful, but are very cathartic and can do a lot of good. Narcissists use emotional energy to abuse. Going no contact cuts off their ability to continue to abuse. It's important to make no contact a time of healing, renewing, and growing. You can direct your emotional pain into passion and energy to transform your life."

Delaney Jessica Kay

In my experience with unhealthy, destructive, abusive relationships, I have learned that we each have a breaking point. We reach a fork in the road in which we must make a major decision. Do we stay to continue the cycle of abuse? Or do we boldly and bravely decide to cut the ties for once and for all?

This is a personal choice. It is not an easy one. It may cause ongoing concerns. No one else can make this choice for you. Only you can determine what is best for you and healthiest for you.

Not making a decision or staying on the fence about ending a toxic relationship is actually a passive decision. It means that you choose to keep the status quo. While it may be on a subconscious level, you gave your power away.

Are you hindering your emotional wellbeing, safety, and future? Even more important, how will this impact your mental health and ability to heal trauma? Staying in a dysfunctional, psychologically abusive relationship will only hurt **you**; not the narcissist and/or perpetrators.

You owe it to yourself to protect yourself from further bullying, manipulation, gaslighting, and abuse. Otherwise, the drama, deception, and abuse will continue. You can't fix them. You cannot make them see your viewpoint. The only person who you have control over is yourself.

Therefore, it is up to you to make realistic changes to improve your quality of life. There's that saying, if you keep doing what you have been doing, nothing will change. It's unproductive and a waste of your precious energy. Please consider your safety and future.

You have three realistic choices:

1. **Resist Making Changes** – If you don't create positive changes, your circumstances will not change. There's a likely chance that your situation will not improve. You may suffer the long-term consequences of staying in abusive relationships. It can take a negative toll on you, your mental and physical health, your happiness, and your quality of life.
2. **Practice the Grey Rock Method** – This involves limiting your communication and time spent with toxic people. You reduce phone calls, text messages, visits, and all forms of

communication with the narcissist and flying monkeys. The key is to not give them an emotional reaction when they intentionally push your buttons. Keep in mind, they will do everything within their human ability to bait you, upset you, gaslight you, and bully you. They know exactly how to tick you off. They love when you fight back with them. Therefore, don't fight back. Ignore them. Don't engage with them.

3. **Go No Contact** – When you go no contact with the narcissist and flying monkeys, this means that you are not in communication with them at all. There are no phone calls, no text messaging, no following them on social media or responding to their social media posts, no writing letters to them, no visiting them, no attending social functions where they are at, including baby showers, graduations, weddings, birthdays, holidays, funerals, or family gatherings. You opt out of seeing them; face to face and online. No contact is called estrangement when it is your family of origin. The average person who chooses to go no contact didn't do this impulsively. It was never spontaneous. Rather, it was the last resort to break free from narcissistic abuse and destructive relationships.

The Grey Rock Method: A Foolproof Technique to Shut Down Toxic People

Most scapegoats and abuse survivors are kind, caring, conscientious people. They are typically empaths and/or Highly Sensitive People who try to surround themselves with positive, drama-free folks. It's not always possible to cut out every single toxic person from your life. This is when the grey rock method comes in handy.

It is a realistic way to do damage control when you're dealing with tough personalities, especially a narcissist, flying monkeys, the trouble-maker at work, your jealous siblings, your sociopathic parent, or your energy vampire ex-spouse. Here's the lowdown on grey rock.

According to the website, MindFool.com, "***The grey rock technique** is an effective method to get the toxic person in your life to lose interest in you. Especially when cutting off a person is not possible due to various reasons. You instead apply a strategy that makes them choose to be distant from you instead of the other way round. Instead of cutting full contact with a toxic person, you allow contact. But you respond to their drama with boring and monotonous replies. This makes you less attractive in the eyes of a drama-seeker. And they will eventually get tired of getting desirable responses from you. That's when they will move on looking for more interesting people who can satisfy and fuel their need for drama. Them leaving you out of their network is the best thing that can happen to you.*"

THE MAIN GOAL of using the grey rock method is to enable a smooth transition from being close to being more distant with a toxic person in your life. **Tips for the grey rock method:**

1. **Don't Reveal Your Strategy** – Avoid telling the toxic people what you are up to. If you slip up and admit that you are 'grey rocking,' the narcissist and other bullies will amp up their covert schemes. Trust me on this, you don't want anyone to know what you are doing. Why? Because it could lead to more smear campaigns, retaliation, and outright violence. If the emotional vampires are onto you, they may seek revenge in effort to harm you, to destroy your reputation, your career, and your entire life.
2. **Don't Divulge Personal Information** – Usually, the narc and/or flying monkeys will constantly be watching you. They may ask you intrusive, personal questions. Be careful about what you say to them. Anything you feed them becomes ammunition they can use against you. Never confide in them about your personal problems. Do not tell them about your love life, health, work, children/grandchildren, if you're moving, if you are dating, if you've had a salary increase, or if you're struggling. When it comes to untrustworthy people, less is more. Toxic and manipulative people thrive on conflict, drama, and chaos. Give them nothing. If they pry into your personal space or ask you questions that you can't avoid, keep your facial expression blank. Don't give an emotional reaction to them. Keep it vague and bland. Try replying with "mm-hmm" or "uh-huh," rather than a long explanation. Remember the JADE technique; don't justify yourself, argue, defend yourself, or try to explain yourself.
3. **Limit Contact & Communication** – Just because your narcissistic ex-spouse sends you hateful messages, you don't have to react or respond to him/her. You can ignore it, document it for legal records, take a screenshot of it, and carry on. Don't ask how they are doing. Don't inquire about

their health or what's going on in their life. Good chance, they will fabricate stories and you will never get the truth from them. Limit contact with them. This includes visits, phone calls, text messages, emails, social media messages, and limiting your social time with these particular people. Keep all forms of contact with abusers short and brief. If necessary, say, *"I have an appointment or I need to go."* Then immediately hang up the phone before they can swindle you into a conflict.

4. **Stay Distracted & Detached** - Another helpful technique when using the grey rock method is to remain distracted and emotionally detached. You can try carrying a book, using your cellphone, or simply keeping your mind focused on your favorite person or pet. This not only helps create some emotional distance, but can also make it easier to weather the storm if the person escalates their attempts to engage you by saying cruel or hurtful words. It can be difficult to not defend yourself when you feel attacked. Ultimately, you'll reduce the damage by not engaging. Emotional detachment serves to undermine a narcissist's attempts to lure you in and to manipulate you, causing them to grow uninterested and bored. It works in your favor to become dull, boring, monotonous, and humdrum.
5. **Disconnect** – Avoid eye contact with the instigators when practicing the grey rock method. The reason why is because eye contact helps facilitate an emotional connection. Rather than look into their eyes, focus on another activity, look elsewhere, play with your cellphone, or find creative ways to avoid all eye contact with the abusers. This is an easy way to reinforce your sense of emotional disconnection and detachment to them.
6. **Avoid 'You' Statements** – When you have no choice, but to speak to a narcissist or flying monkeys, avoid 'you' statements, such as *"You hurt me badly," "You cheated on me,"* or *"You lied to me."* They can become quite defensive. Avoiding these

statements is helpful if you are still in a relationship with a toxic person.

Have you ever wondered why people choose the grey rock method, instead of no contact? In some situation's there are good reasons for staying in contact with the narcissist and/or flying monkeys. If you are separated or divorced from your ex-narcissist, you may have no choice in this, especially if you and your ex have children together.

While your children are young or teenagers, grey rock may be necessary. For at least 18 years, or until your children become independent adults, you and your spouse will be co-parenting. Although this can be unpleasant, stressful, and may involve them manipulating you, try to follow the tips up above to grey rock.

Another reason some folks practice grey rock is because they have strict religious or cultural beliefs. In some counties, there are ethnic and/or religious practices in which you may be forced to stay in a toxic relationship with your narcissistic parent, sibling, spouse, and/or relatives. If this is your situation, focus on the JADE technique. Practice the grey rock tips to maintain your safe space and sanity.

Lastly, if you are in an intimate relationship with a partner or spouse and you don't have the financial freedom to move out on your own, you may need to grey rock. It's very common for women to feel trapped in an abusive relationship or marriage if they are broke or lack financial independence. Oftentimes, narcissistic spouses do abuse their wives by hoarding money. Typically, the victim has no access to the bank account, checkbook, credit cards, or any finances. If this is your reason for staying in an unhappy and very destructive relationship, your option is to practice grey rock, rather than go no contact.

In my past experience, I didn't know about the grey rock method in 1990 when I started using it. My husband and I were newlyweds when I discovered that his grandmother, Mary, despised my mother-in-law. Mary would constantly call me and spread terrible rumors about my husband's mom. After a few years of this nonsense, I couldn't take the negativity any longer. I actually did grey rock with Mary without knowing about grey rock. I stopped calling her, seeing her, and did my best to limit all contact with Mary.

At a wedding in 1991, Mary approached me and verbally lashed out at me. Her words were so offensive, spiteful, and hostile. Instantly, my skin all over my body broke out into hives. It was a physical reaction to Mary, a very toxic, psychologically abusive woman. Long story short, being in Mary's presence caused me to become physically ill; a manifestation of negative energy from an emotional vampire. I opted out and left the wedding. I don't regret my decision. I believe that I intuitively knew what was best for me, my mental wellbeing, and my physical health.

Fast forward to 2018 when I realized that my mom and siblings were very offensive towards me. At this time in my life, I had already spent decades trying to grey rock with them. While I may not have understood everything about grey rock, I did limit all contact with my mother and sisters.

My mom noticed that I stopped visiting her as much. She constantly nagged me about it. She complained, *"You don't spend time with me anymore. I rarely hear from you or see you."* Instead of trying to explain myself or to justify myself to her, I had no expression on my face. I nonchalantly stated, *"I have a full plate."*

As time went by, my mom still badgered me about not going out with her or seeing her as much as I used to, I quit responding altogether. I would shrug my shoulders or stay silent. At this stage of my codependent relationship with my mom, I had no energy left to give her. I had no more words, no more time, and no more excuses to give her. Therefore, I said nothing.

The truth is that I stopped caring about her when she continued to mistreat me. I stopped caring about toxic family members who clearly did not care about me, my life, my dreams, my health, my career, my marriage, and my children.

Sometimes, healing from narcissistic abuse means to stop putting energy into relationships that are already broken. Those relationships were already dead. After exhausting all attempts to salvage the unpleasant relationships, I had no more to give. I felt exhausted and fatigued from countless decades of grey rocking.

For me, the grey rock method was an epic failure. This is my personal experience. Grey rock didn't salvage my peace of mind. Grey rock did not help me to become empowered. Grey rock did not increase my physical, emotional, or spiritual health. Grey rock never diminished my anxiety, my triggers, my flashbacks, my chronic pain, nor my grief and loss.

I can only share what has worked for me and what hasn't worked for me. Keep in mind that what works for one person may not work equally as well for another. Your situation with the narcissist and my circumstances can be very different. Plus, we must consider all of the variables, such as my childhood neglect and abuse, my sexual trauma, my growing up with a dysfunctional family unit, my being an extrovert who is assertive, and my special gifts of having an 'inner knowing,' including intuitiveness.

The Nuts & Bolts of Going No Contact

By July 2018, it was obvious the grey rock technique was unsuccessful for me. After attempting all other options, I came to the understanding that I had to cut ties with my narcissist mother. When I went no contact with her, my sisters freaked out. They started gaslighting me, blame-shifting me, manipulating me, and retaliating against me. Therefore, I instantly went no contact with all of my sisters, their families, and my relatives.

The reality was that they didn't understand me, my situation, nor did they care to try to understand my anguish. Rather, they chose to defend and protect our narcissistic mother. In most dysfunctional families, this is common. Usually, a toxic family unit will gang up on the scapegoat or the black sheep of the family. They won't take responsibility for their own misconduct and transgressions.

I will be the first to admit that I didn't become estranged with my birth family impulsively. No, it wasn't an impulsive or spontaneous decision. Instead, it was well thought out. I prayed about it and took heed when I felt led to cut all ties with them.

Nobody goes no contact with a loving, caring, gentle, safe family. They end toxic relationships because all other alternatives were exhausted and unsuccessful. They broke all connections to abusive people because it was the last resort.

Truly, the relationships were unhealthy and disastrous. They cannot be resurrected. There can't be reconciliation. We cannot restore a destructive relationship with abusive people if they refuse to repent. We cannot repair broken relationships if they won't take ownership of how they intentionally hurt us and if they deny their psychological abuse. We find the strength to release them. We let them go. It is the kindest act of self-preservation, self-love, and self-care. It is precisely how we heal our trauma.

Of course, going no contact does not mean that we don't love them or think about them. It doesn't mean that we are heartless or insensitive. It does not mean that we are awful human beings. What it does mean is that we learn which battles are worth fighting for. We learn which battles and people are worth letting go to improve our emotional wellness and quality of life.

My experience of no contact was a bumpy road. It had many potholes, dips, and unexpected curveballs. After four months of being no contact with my mom and siblings, I started to second-guess myself. During a vulnerable moment, I called my mother and visited her.

For three months, I tried to restore my relationship with my mom. It didn't work. She continued to gaslight me, manipulate me, stonewall me, bully me, and stir up trouble in my life. As I reflect back on this timeline, I sincerely believe that a Higher Power wanted me in communication with my mom for a divine purpose. I have no doubt, God used me as a vessel to minister to my own mother.

On a beautiful autumn day, my mom and I were driving to a local restaurant. I wanted to treat her to a delicious seafood dinner. As I was driving, my mom randomly blurted, *"I think I'm going to hell."*

Surprised by her confession, I inquired, *"What makes you think that?"* My mom mumbled, *"I've made a lot of mistakes. When I die, I'm going to hell."*

Frankly, I understood why she believed that she'd go to hell. Oftentimes, I wondered the same thing. Distressed, I fervently prayed for her. I didn't want my mother to end up in hell or to be tortured in the afterlife.

Gently, I lamented, *"Mother, no one on earth is perfect. We all make mistakes and poor choices. Do you have faith in God? Can you ask Him for forgiveness?"*

Perplexed, my mom replied, *"I don't know. I've tried to pray, but I'm not good at it."*

For the next two days, I visited my mom, I prayed for her. I tried to comfort her. Silently, I felt like I was in a wrestling match. Despite how much hurt and trauma she had inflicted onto me, I wanted her to feel that she was worthy of going heaven. That she could have a positive 'life after death transition.' I sensed an urgency to pray for her soul. Earnestly, I prayed for God to intervene on her behalf.

I never stopped loving my mom. Not when I went no contact the first time, the second time, nor the third time. For me, the process of going full no contact was extremely heartbreaking, stressful, and complicated. It looks like three's a charm! It took me three attempts to finally stick to my healthy boundaries.

After exhausting other alternatives, I understood that I had no other options left. Going no contact with my mom was my last resort. I had to repeatedly remind myself about why I went no contact in the first place. Reading books, blogs, and watching videos about narcissistic abuse helped me to maintain distance.

There is no single reason why someone chooses to cut ties with a narcissist and toxic relationships. There were not only one or two transgressions. Instead, there were hundreds of offenses. There were countless violations. Not only to us, but to our boundaries, self-worth, and dignity.

There were dozens upon dozens of times they had criticized, ostracized, condemned, judged, ridiculed, and mistreated us. Perpetual bullying, manipulating, deceiving, denying, playing the victim card, having selective amnesia, retaliating, stalking us, and crazy-making mind games.

My family estrangement isn't about my not loving my mother, sisters, or relatives. Rather, it's about loving myself enough to break free of toxic, unhealthy family dynamics that crushed my heart and soul. I did what was crucial to start healing my trauma. I have no regrets. I rescued myself.

The No Contact Rule:

- Zero contact; face to face & online
- No phone calls
- No text messaging
- No contact via social media
- No attending social functions where they are at
- No emails
- No letters, cards, or gifts
- No checking their social media profile
- No contacting their family, friends, or co-workers
- No combing through old photographs of them
- No going down memory lane on how it used to be
- No showing up at the same parties, weddings, or concerts
- No keeping old pictures, cards, or letters from them
- No stopping by their place to pick up your stuff
- No communication at all
- No hanging out at the places you used to spend together

No matter how brutal, challenging, and painful it can feel, this is for your own mental health. If you really want to break free from narcissistic abuse and heal your trauma, it will take effort. No contact will require you to become consistent in staying no contact. This doesn't mean that it's smooth sailing. That is the furthest from the truth.

Going no contact is hard. Staying and maintaining no contact is even harder. With time, patience, and your willingness to keep a long distance from the narcissist and/or abusers, you will eventually experience awesome benefits. You notice that you are not as stressed out. Your anxiety and depression may decrease. You find yourself happier, laughing, and enjoying your life. You start to focus on gratitude and become more aware of your blessings. You feel peace wash over you. It's the best thing on earth!

For some people, this transition can take months. For others, it can take years to get used to being estranged from the narcissist and flying monkeys. The more emotional support you have in place, the smoother your transition into full no contact can be. I strongly advocate for seeking emotional support through trusted friends, family, a support group, a trauma-informed therapist, and/or an experienced Certified Trauma Recovery Coach.

Recently, I read this inspiring quote on Twitter by an Empath named Lawson Peterson. It is spot on and I resonate with it. *"If you were born in an unconscious family or, a huge part of your purpose is to break those generational cycles and reclaim your power and free will. It's not going to be easy. It wasn't meant to be. You'll need to question the toxic patterns and the dysfunction of the people you grew up around, and have the courage to see the truth of it all, without sugarcoating or gaslighting any aspect of yourself. These very dark experiences act as tools for your ascension and evolution because by facing what you don't want, you become clearer on what's the highest aligned."*

10 Tips to Go No Contact:

1. **Toxic People & Toxic Environment** – You can't fully heal if you stay involved with a toxic person. You cannot recover from trauma if you remain in the toxic environment that made you sick. The reason most people go no contact is because they clearly get it. They come to realize that these destructive people will never change. Therefore, they opt to release all toxic people and environments in order to start their healing journey.
2. **Trust Your Intuition** – If something in the back of your mind is alerting you to danger or to unhealthy dynamics in your relationships, take heed. Don't ignore it, dismiss it, or minimize it. Trust your gut instincts. Know that your emotions and intuition are valid. If you sense it's time to let go of a toxic person, do it. Take action.

3. **Skip Closure** – In most abusive relationships, when it ends there is no closure. This applies to the black sheep of the family and the scapegoat. Typically, after you go no contact with someone, you won't have closure. There will be loose ends hanging. You may need to resist the urge to get closure from the abuser. At some point in your healing journey, you may need to actively release trying to find closure. There will be no heart-to-heart chat about what went wrong in your relationship. The narcissist will not take ownership for how badly they hurt you. He or she will not confess to their wrongdoing, their secret affair, or how they inflicted pain in your life. You will not get logical explanations, nor truthful answers. Your toxic relationship was messy, confusing, painful, and emotionally draining.
4. **Don't Fall for Flying Monkey Tactics** – When you go no contact with the narcissist, it's common for a narcissist to recruit flying monkeys. The flying monkeys will try to contact you to get the 'dirt' on you. They will try to pressure you, stir up drama, discord, stalk you, provoke you, bully you, retaliate against you, lie about you, and spread horrible rumors about you. Beware of their evil tactics. Don't fall for it.
5. **Healthy Boundaries** – Either before or after you go no contact, it's crucial to set clear, healthy boundaries. Your personal and professional boundaries are the limits that you set for yourself. They protect your sense of personal identity and help to guard against being overwhelmed by the unrealistic demands of others. Boundaries are vital because they prevent you from becoming enmeshed in toxic relationships. The first step to build better boundaries is to get a clear understanding of your relationship dynamics, what is healthy for you, and what your limits involve. Your boundaries are about you and your standards. It's not about other people.
6. **No Assumptions about Toxic People** – Do not assume the narcissist and perpetrators will respect you, your boundaries,

especially after you cut ties with them. In most cases, they will repeatedly disrespect you, your boundaries, and your no contact rule. They will try to find ways to slip back into your life. Don't assume they won't show up at your doorstep, send you hate mail, or they may even stoop so low to call the police on you. Many of my clients and YouTube viewers, have shared how the narc plays nasty tricks on them after they went grey rock or no contact with them. Therefore, don't have high expectations of cruel people. Instead, expect the unexpected. By all means, if you feel threatened or unsafe, call your local authorities ASAP.

7. **Be Firm** - Once you've made up your mind to go no contact, you will endure every narcissistic trick in the book. They will try to make you feel guilty. They will deny your feelings. They will send you pleading emails, begging you to contact them. They will do a very good impression of behaving like an emotionally healthy person if they think it will make you change your mind. The one thing they won't do, however, is take an honest look at themselves and their behavior. The narcissist and abusers will not change. They can cry wolf all they want. At the end of the day, they still remain abusive, evil people. Therefore, be firm and be confident in your decision to end the hurtful relationship.
8. **Rebuild Your Life** – Many studies have proven that the more active you are to rebuild a new life, the better you will feel. Consider new hobbies, take a class, meet new people, get physically fit, tap into your creativity, do what you love, and take realistic action steps to improve your overall life. For some people, they change their hairstyle, get a new color, jazz up their fashion, or join a gym. For others, they may relocate out of state, move into a new home, gain new skills, join a meet up group, rescue a pet for companionship, start playing an instrument, or make meaningful online connections with likeminded folks. The goal is to make positive changes in your life; personally, relationally, professionally, emotionally,

spiritually, physically, and/or artistically. Whatever sets your heart on fire, go for it!

9. **Self-care** – Once you are no contact, I suggest increasing your self-care practices. For each person, it can look differently because we each have unique likes and interests. Self-care is essential for your mental health, emotional wellbeing, your relationships, your health, and your physical wellness. Some people enjoy golfing, swimming, or getting involved with sports. For others, it may be relaxing in the sunshine outdoors, listening to your favorite tunes, dancing, drawing, gardening, sewing, cooking gourmet meals, or using pure essential oils for grounding, calming, and emotionally supporting yourself.
10. **Surround Yourself with a Good Support Network** – Now more than ever, you will need a good support network. It can be your adult children, spouse, partner, friend, relatives, clergy, online or in person support group, a licensed counselor, psychologist, or a Certified Trauma Recovery Coach. Being no contact can be difficult. It's even harder if you have to do it without emotional support. It's essential to have caring people in your life who understand what you have experienced. Those who support you 100%. Join a support group for Adult Children of Narcissistic Parents/Spouse or start one of your own. But be careful who you tell. People who haven't been raised by a narcissist or married to one may see your decision as cruel or an overreaction. Not everyone understands how unhealthy the abusive family system and/or toxic relationships are. You don't need to deal with other's judgments of you, particularly if they can't personally relate to what you have experienced.

TWELVE

Build Better Boundaries

"When it comes to boundaries, most victims of abuse are a bit shaky on setting boundaries to protect themselves. As a child of a narcissist, I never learned to set boundaries. I never knew I could say, 'No, I am not comfortable with that request.' When we are dealing with a narcissist, they test us. They push your personal boundaries to see how much they can abuse you."

Tracy A. Malone

When you were a child or teen, were you taught to set boundaries? Did your parent, relatives, or teachers model healthy boundaries? As an adult, have you implemented personal boundaries?

As a child, teen, and young adult, I wasn't taught boundaries. My mother didn't have boundaries. She never modeled it, nor practiced it. Instead, she pushed every single button of mine. She disrespected me. She treated me like I was an unworthy object; not a special human being.

Her unspoken message to me: *"You have no value. You're not important. Obey my rules or you will suffer the consequences. Do as I say, not as I do."*

In my work as a Certified Trauma Recovery Coach, I know it's hard for some survivors to set clear boundaries. Please know this is a normal and common trauma response. Abuse survivors were taught lies about what's right and wrong. Oftentimes, we've come to accept unhealthy and abnormal behaviors to be normal. In reality, they are abnormal. Yet, it's all we have known.

Through brainwashing, gaslighting, and manipulation, we've been taught four lies:

1. You are a bad person.
2. The abuse was your fault.
3. You should be ashamed of yourself.
4. You are powerless.

Dear Beautiful Souls, it's time to dismantle the lies that you were brainwashed to believe. They are not true. Even if the perpetrators didn't take accountability, they are responsible for what they said and did to you. You are not meant to carry a heavy burden of toxic shame, guilt, or blame for what the narcissist or perpetrators had inflicted upon you.

May you know you are deserving to be treated with tenderness, dignity, compassion, empathy, and love. Your personal boundaries should be respected by others. Most survivors have experienced the narcissist and flying monkeys who disregarded their boundaries. Oftentimes, they punished you for setting healthy boundaries. They push back. They don't take 'no' for an answer. I've experienced this by my mom, sisters, and relative's numerous times.

In effort to understand boundaries, let's first define what it is. According to Wikipedia, *"Personal boundaries are guidelines, rules, or limits that a person creates to identify reasonable, safe, and permissible ways for other people to behave towards them and how they will respond when someone passes those limits."*

Our boundaries are not about other people. Rather, it is about us and our perimeters. We set our own standards. We determine what is right or inappropriate for us. We set our limits on what types of behaviors we accept and what isn't tolerable.

Psychology Today defines boundaries as *"An invisible line you draw around yourself to identify what is acceptable behavior."*

Healthy boundaries are a line between two people. For each person, this can look different. Each one of us may have our own set of guidelines for what we permit versus what we will not permit by another person.

For those who were raised in a dysfunctional family where you may have experienced bullying, gaslighting, manipulation, and abuse, there are higher chances that your parent's or caregiver did not teach you about healthy boundaries. Therefore, as a child and/or teenager, you were not aware of boundaries, due to lack of having a role model. For many of my clients and YouTube viewers, it was not until they were an adult when they set better boundaries.

Various Forms of Healthy Boundaries:

1. **Physical Boundaries** – This relates to your personal space, privacy, and your body. For example, some people who may stand too close to you or get in your face are sign of overstepping your boundaries. Another example is when children are told to hug a relative or stranger, such as an uncle who they barely know. It may feel quite uncomfortable to the child and cause them great distress.
2. **Emotional Boundaries** – This is a limit that protects ourselves from manipulation, mistreatment, and being hurt. An emotional boundary is standing up for your beliefs, values, thoughts, and morals. It is a healthy expression of our self-respect, self-worth, and dignity.
3. **Financial Boundaries** – This is how you save, spend, give,

earn, and budget your money. A healthy financial boundary in a marriage is freely opening up your own bank account, especially if you have a professional business. When a spouse or partner refuses to let you have your own bank account, credit cards, or your own money, it is a red flag for overstepping your financial boundaries. It is financial abuse.

4. **Online Boundaries** – This is important for social media, emails, text messages, and the internet. It seems like no one talks about this topic. Yet, how many of us are being silenced, censored, bullied, stalked, and verbally attacked online? An example of a healthy online boundary is to not participate in hurtful and cruel comments, especially on social media. My personal online boundaries for my YouTube channel do require me to first review all comments before they go live. On my YouTube channel, I don't approve of negative, hostile, or cruel comments. If someone writes a malicious, offensive, mean-spirited remark, I report them, block them, and carry on.
5. **Sexual Boundaries** – This means that you have specific rules pertaining to your comfort level around physical touch, intimacy, affection, your physical body, and sexual behaviors. An example of someone crossing your line of sexual boundaries is when you meet someone new and they instantly start asking you for nude pictures or private messaging you their own nude pics. It's inappropriate.
6. **Spiritual Boundaries** – Each person has their own personal beliefs about organized religion. Not everyone has the same upbringing, understanding, educational background, religious beliefs, or spiritual beliefs as others. Some folks believe in God, while others may believe in a Higher Creator, or something totally different. Religious gaslighting is when someone uses the Bible, verses, or God as a weapon to hurt you, to shame you, to condemn you, and to ostracize you. For example, on social media, I've seen so-called Christian's demand abuse survivors 'forgive the sexual predator' or

'forgive your father for physically abusing you.' This is rude, insulting, and repulsive. It's not up to anyone else on whether you forgive the abuser, predator, or narcissist. It's your life. Your choice. Only you can make the best decision for yourself. A person named Autumn Shroud sums up this toxic mindset about forgiveness. He said, *"The concept of forgiveness allows the abuser to still abuse, and keeps the victim in a constant state of victimhood."*

Common Reasons for Unhealthy Boundaries

Perhaps, you were not taught healthy boundaries as a child or young adult? Your needs and wants may have been ignored, denied, ridiculed, or minimized. Do you find yourself people-pleasing in effort to keep the peace? You don't want to offend anyone. You prefer to go with the flow. You may try to avoid conflicts. You may fear standing up for yourself. You may avoid speaking up when other's hurt you.

Another reason you may not have built better boundaries is because you were raised by an abusive parent, caregiver, or narcissist. It may have been one or more narcissistic parents, a grandparent, or a toxic sibling who bullied you. Most narcissistic parents expect that all of their needs and wants are met, despite how unrealistic it is to expect that from a child or teen.

Lastly, you may have suffered intense abuse by your intimate partner, spouse, or friend who's a narcissist. They may have insisted you 'submit' to them. The covert narcissist may have ridiculed you, condemned you, silenced you, and psychologically tormented you for so long that you couldn't set boundaries for yourself. Or even if you did have boundaries, the narcissist incessantly violated them.

How to Create Healthy Boundaries:

1. Educate yourself about healthy boundaries.
2. Determine what your limits and rules are for yourself.
3. Be aware of the signs when someone crossed your boundaries.
4. Learn to bravely speak up if someone oversteps your boundaries.
5. It is perfectly fine to say 'no' to someone who isn't in alignment with your morals, values, lifestyle, and beliefs.
6. Release feeling guilty for creating boundaries. There is nothing to be guilty or ashamed of. It's for your own protection and peace of mind.
7. Be clear in what you ask for and what you want or need.
8. Seek emotional support.
9. Learn to express your authentic emotions even if you disagree with someone or when you have your own unique perspective. Understand that not everyone will respect your boundaries. You do have permission to show them to the door.
10. Trust your gut instincts and body signals that are alerting you of potential danger. Listen to that soft voice within you that guides you to safety.

Creating better boundaries is a super power! It puts you back in the driver's seat of your life. You become the CEO for your standards and limits.

Healing Trauma Requires Self-care

> *"Self-care is never a selfish act – it is simply good stewardship of the only gift I have, the gift I was put on earth to offer others. Anytime we can listen to true self and give the care it requires, we do it not only for ourselves, but for the many others whose lives we touch."*

Looking back on the process of my trauma recovery to regain my health and emotional wellbeing, it required self-care. Not just occasionally, but on a consistent daily basis. According to Dictionary.com, self-care is *"Care of the self without medical or other professional consultation."* From my experience, self-care is actively engaging in the productive activities that may help us to maintain optimal wellness; to enhance our body, emotions, and spiritual health.

Self-care is doing what we can do with what we have on a consistent basis to improve our whole being. This proactive approach can place us in a better position to heal. To go from barely surviving to thriving!

Over the course of two decades, when I consider how I got from there to here, it wasn't one particular method helping me along my healing path. Rather, it was multiple therapeutic, self-care strategies, which proved highly beneficial. My overall condition improved from being disabled and homebound to becoming healthier and independent. (For the full story, read my memoir, *Soul Cry: Releasing & Healing the Wounds of Trauma.*)

This doesn't mean I'm 'cured' of fibromyalgia, narcissistic abuse, sexual assaults, CPTSD, and compounded trauma. It means that despite my challenges, I've gained better insight to lead a higher quality of life. More so, I actively sought practical life-style changes to improve my physical, emotional, and spiritual wellbeing. Each one was like finding a missing piece of a puzzle, which gradually led to my restoration.

In a nutshell, self-care is an empowering expression of *self-love.* Despite our failings and weaknesses, we learn to love ourselves and view ourselves as worthy. We care for our inner child. We learn to mother our own selves. We appreciate ourselves in such a positive way that we flourish.

During my darkest and gloomiest moments, self-love was not easy. It wasn't automatic. Having emotional dysregulation and triggers came easier for me. I've learned the hard way that how I respond to stress greatly influences my health; for better or for worse. Caring for oneself and loving oneself requires diligence. It can evolve through time.

Self-care & Self-love:

- Loving ourselves means taking good care of our body, mind, & soul.
- Caring for ourselves is not selfish.
- Self-care & self-love require being true to ourselves.
- By being true to oneself, we create healthy boundaries.
- We let go of people-pleasing.
- We listen to our body's signals to eat, sleep, reduce stress, be still, etc.
- We follow our intuition.
- No rehashing past mistakes, experiences, or regrets that can hinder our progress.
- We take responsibility for our own words, behaviors, & actions.
- We seek wisdom, discernment, & ask God/Higher Power for guidance.
- We don't seek permission to be ourselves.
- We give our body the nurturing, rest, exercise, & comfort it needs.
- We are honest with ourselves about our strengths & weaknesses.
- We take time to grow spiritually & connect to a Higher Power on a deeper level.
- We feel our emotions without berating ourselves or feeling guilty.

- We strive for self-improvement and accept ourselves where we are now.

Consciously, we choose to give ourselves the gift of self-care. To honor, respect, and love the precious life in which we've been blessed with, including the good, the bad, and the downright painful. It's an enriching process of self-growth that can lead to acceptance.

We may not like how we look or feel right now, but we can come to terms with it. We may despise our triggers, flashbacks, emotional meltdowns, or our trauma wounds, yet we go beyond the superficial to love and care for ourselves fully.

Regardless of our age, gender, or season in life, at some point we may find ourselves carrying heavy burdens. Extra stress. Broken relationships. Painful betrayal. Grief and loss. Illnesses. Disappointments. Isolation. Narcissistic abuse. The list is endless. Any which we look at it, carrying heavy burdens, especially over a lengthy period of time, can take a toll on us. To move forward to healing, it will entail self-care.

Before I explain practical steps to achieve self-care, let's first cover the basics of what self-care does not involve. **Self-care is not:**

- Getting intoxicated with alcohol
- Indulging in street drugs
- Abusing pharmaceutical medications
- Numbing out with chemicals
- Living in a toxic environment
- Self-harming or injury
- Binging & purging
- Destructive behaviors or lifestyles
- Neglecting your safety and/or health
- Staying in toxic, destructive relationships

Self-care is a set of practices that help you feel nourished. Self-care is taking time to refresh, renew, and recharge in a manner that is meaningful to you. Based on the fact that we each have our own likes and dislikes as well as unique personalities, self-care may differ from person to person. For example, an introvert may desire to be alone and rest for self-care whereas an extrovert may want to be in a social environment and active during self-care.

As for myself, I've always been a social butterfly as an extrovert. However, during my initial recovery process in 2018 when I upgraded my boundaries and went no contact with my mom, I needed to take time out from the chaos. In order to be true to myself and honor the dark place where I was at (narcissistic abuse), I accepted my difficult season. I had hope to recover.

One eye-opening quote that I read hit home for me. It's by an author, trauma expert, teacher, and psychiatrist, Judith Lewis Herman. She wrote, *"Many abused children cling to the hope that growing up will bring escape and freedom. But the personality formed in the environment of coercive control is not well adapted to adult life. The survivor is left with fundamental problems in basic trust, autonomy, and initiative. She approaches the task of early adulthood – establishing independence and intimacy – burdened by major impairments of self-care, in cognition and memory, in identity, and in the capacity to form stable relationships. She is still a prisoner of her childhood; attempting to create a new life, she reencounters the trauma."* (The excerpt is from Herman's book, *Trauma and Recovery: The Aftermath of Violence – From Domestic Abuse to Political Terror)*

My Unique Stages of Healing & Self-care Involved:

- **Journaling** - In search of peace, I journaled. I've been doing this since I was a young girl. It feels freeing to release all of my hurt, frustrations, and baggage. Journaling gave me the opportunity to vent, cry, and ponder the bumpy road I've traveled. Expressing my inner thoughts and feelings were a godsend. With pen and paper in hand, I ranted about my harrowing trials, my abusive siblings, and my narc mom. It felt good to let go of negative energy. I poured out my heart on paper. I wrote my deepest dreams and aspirations. Most importantly, journaling provided positive benefits by reducing stress, clarifying thoughts, effectively solving problems, exploring my strengths, praying, and increasing my awareness of my hidden blessings. Journaling became a blissful sanctuary. A safe place to be real. No pressure or worry about being harshly judged. It brought calm to my storm. New insight. Peace of mind. Personal growth. This amazing form of self-care powerfully awakened my inner voice. Ultimately, it helped me to reconnect to my inner child who needed me to rescue her. Today, we lovingly walk hand in hand.

- **Gratitude** – In effort to improve my outlook on life, I started compiling a list of things that I was grateful for. Cultivating an attitude of gratitude begins with counting our blessings. Gratitude is expressing thanks for special blessings we receive. When life gets hectic or we feel overwhelmed, we can take a moment to focus on the people or situations we are most grateful for. When we have an attitude of gratitude other things will fall by the wayside. The more we are grateful for what we have, the more we can live fully in the present moment. When we live in the present moment, the greater we build stepping stones for a brighter future. Being thankful helps us to take into account all of the positive in our lives. It gives us a whole new perspective.
- **Soothing Sounds** - During long nights when I was plagued with insomnia, I dimmed the lights and listened to soft music, which promoted relaxation. One CD combined flowing, ethereal music with soothing sounds of waves lapping against the shore. Closing my eyes, I was magically transported to a tropical island where I could envision sea gulls soaring

overhead, feel the warm sun radiating on my skin, and envision myself walking barefoot on the beach. A cool breeze ruffled through my hair as I knelt down to pick up a beautiful sea shell. As I listened to its tranquil sound of ocean waves, blissful peace gently washed over me. Other musical options included soothing soundtracks of calming atmospheres, strings, piano, and guitar. For stress relief, some people enjoy nature music with the soft pitter-patter of raindrops, birds singing, or flowing waterfalls. While your preference may vary, choose a style of soothing sounds that resonates within your own spirit.

- **Tranquility & Aromatherapy** – Sometimes when I felt sad, anxious, or restless, I created a relaxing environment by lighting candles or diffusing pure essential oils to encourage solitude. My favorite scents for aromatherapy were Lavender essential oil (relaxing & stress reliever), Bergamot essential oil (calming & uplifting), and Wild Orange (joy & peace). If my fibromyalgia flared, I'd soak in a hot bathtub filled with Epsom salts and a few drops of Lavender essential oil. It was very common for me to light scented candles around the tub to simply relish in the tranquil atmosphere. In my experience, this form of self-care made a world of difference; physically and mentally.
- **Home Spa** – A sure way to lift my spirits and help me to feel better about myself is personal self-care; otherwise known as girly girl pampering. It's amazing how a little bit of lip gloss, flat ironing my hair, and a pedicure dramatically transformed me from feeling blah to exuberant. I'm a huge believer that when we physically look better, we emotionally feel better. Taking time for personal hygiene and adding a little pampering into my self-care routine most definitely boosted my attitude and self-confidence.
- **Positive Affirmations** – At first, this felt a bit awkward for me, but I started saying positive affirmations out loud or writing them down on index cards as little reminders that I

was healing. An affirmation is a statement or phrase that we declare is true. The purpose of verbally saying daily affirmations is to motivate, encourage, and transform our subconscious minds. It's a form of manifesting our deepest desires to become our conscious reality. Regardless of the physical world, we state what we desire the outcome to be. It's kind of like faith; being sure of what we hope for and certain of what we do not see. I woke up in the morning and affirmed, *"I am emotionally supported and protected," "I am divinely loved,"* or *"I am grateful to be healthy, happy, and whole."* Verbally, I affirmed, *"Peace, prosperity, and abundance easily and swiftly flows into my life. And it is done."* For those who battle pessimism or negative self-talk with the inner critic, the kindest act of self-care you can provide for yourself is to speak positive affirmations into your life. Consider learning about The Law of Assumption by Neville Goddard. While it can take effort, speaking positive affirmations and taking power over your own thoughts/beliefs can increase your self-worth, mindset, prosperity, abundance, health, and overall frame of mind.

- **Clean Nutrition** – Along my wellness journey, it became very clear that I needed to clean up my diet to improve my moods, memory, and physical health. I learned about specific foods and drinks that helped me to decrease my inflammation, digestive issues, and fibromyalgia pain. Through time and consistency, I gained wisdom, knowledge, and insight into the truth about genetically modified organisms (GMO), artificial sweeteners, processed foods, and how it affected how I functioned on a day-to-day basis. It's worked wonders for me!

I'm not sure how to tactfully write this? I hope that you will receive it with openness and love. We cannot go through life neglecting self-care by beating up our bodies with nicotine, alcohol, drugs, toxic behaviors, abusive relationships, unhealthy lifestyles, destructive addictions, and chronic stress without reaping long-term, negative results. Along our life journey, our choices do have a significant impact on our future.

The good news is you can start over. You can have a second chance. You can actively increase the quality of your health; physically, emotionally, and spiritually. When you take good care of yourself, you are in a better position to take better care of others. While there are only a certain number of hours in each day and you may have responsibilities, it's important that you carve out special time to focus on your self-care. *You* are worth it!

The main purpose of self-care is to nurture yourself. To take time to replenish your body, mind, and soul. To build awareness of your physical, emotional, and spiritual needs. To advocate for vibrant health. Self-care is not merely existing on earth or barely surviving. Rather, self-care is *intentionally* taking the best care of yourself in order to transform your life to fully thrive.

> *"Rest and self-care are so important. When you take time to replenish your spirit, it allows you to serve others from the overflow. You cannot serve from an empty vessel."*
>
> Eleanor Brown

THIRTEEN

Narcissistic Abuse & a Spiritual Awakening

"Through spiritual maturity you will see new ways to avoid unnecessary suffering; wiser ways to endure unavoidable hardships with grace, and opportunities to turn your pain into lessons of service and healing for others. Your hard journey has had a great purpose! Your pain was always a part of a plan to open your heart to love. Have faith. A miracle is happening in your life; the miracle of pain is transforming you to your highest self."

Bryant H. McGill

For those who've suffered trauma or narcissistic abuse, have you experienced a spiritual awakening? Was there a subtle shift in your beliefs, perception, and mindset?

When I talk about spirituality, I am not referring to organized religion, nor church. There is a big difference between religion and spirituality. It's like night and day. Spirituality and religion are two totally different topics. They are not the same.

By the way, there is no right or wrong way. If you are a church-goer, that is fine. If you are involved with organized religion, great. If you have chosen to not practice religion or if you quit church, that is also perfectly fine. If you consider yourself a spiritually enlightened person, awesome. May we each respect one another's choices.

There is no judgement here. We are each on a unique healing path. For some, it may include spirituality. For others, it may involve going to church or a place of worship. My spiritual journey may not look like yours. And yours may not appear similar to mine. May we offer one another grace, compassion, and respect as we venture new horizons.

The goal is not be stagnant in old patterns or rigid thoughts. To not stay stuck in false, limiting, outworn beliefs. The main goal is to always be stretching ourselves. To leave our comfort zone. To live. To learn. To be willing and open to other teachings and philosophies. We are each still in a process to experience new perspectives each day.

What causes a spiritual awakening? It can be sparked by anything. It can be a completely mundane process or a life-altering experience. It can be spontaneous or out-of-the-blue. A spiritual awakening is mostly triggered by major life changes or traumas, such as a life-threatening illness, accident, mid-life crises, or a hellish ordeal by a narcissist.

This means a spiritual awakening can happen when you lose your job, move away from home, suffer an accident, lose a loved one through death, when you go through a divorce, or when you go no contact with toxic people.

Ultimately, anything that encourages you or even forces you to look at your life from a more spiritual perspective and to build conscious awareness can set you on a path toward a spiritual awakening. At the heart of spirituality is that we are not a physical body with a soul. Rather, we are a soul with a physical body.

Everything that you experience physically, emotionally, spiritually, and relationally has a special gift for you. It is an invitation to see the big picture. To seek a fresh, new viewpoint. To shift your attitude and outlook.

To release 'why' abuse and trauma happened to you. This invitation is a gift to explore how you can learn from each experience; both positive and negative. No matter how grueling, painful, and devastating your trauma can feel, there is a valuable lesson to learn. Are you open to receive nuggets of wisdom?

The wisdom is a gift to process your pain. The gift of listening to your inner child. The gift of holding safe space for your inner child to heal. The gift of knowledge that comes from accepting what you had no control of, especially as a child or teen.

The gift of releasing people, places, and things that have deeply hurt you. The gift of coming home to yourself; physically, emotionally, and spiritually. The gift to reconnect to who you were designed to be. Your birthright is to be loved, to be whole, and to continue to expand yourself.

For each person, spirituality may not appear the same. Each of us have come from a totally different background, belief system, upbringings, and unique perspectives about what soul growth means to us. For you, spirituality may be connected to a Higher Power, the Creator, God, the universe, or something else.

What is a spiritual awakening? According to WakeupWorld.com, *"When we undergo a spiritual awakening, we literally 'wake up' to life. We question our old beliefs, habits, and social conditioning, and we see that there is more to life than how much we have been taught."*

In the rest of this chapter, I will share my spiritual awakening. Then I will list the ten signs that you are experiencing a spiritual awakening. From 2016 through 2018, I had a gradual shift in my conscious reality. Slowly, I started to build more awareness about my own soul growth.

Some people may have thought my experience was a 'faith crisis.' Nope, it was not. Instead, I was truly awakened to my core essence. To understand my soul mission in life. To know that I am not a physical body having a spiritual experience, but I am a spiritual being having a physical experience on earth. This nudged me to release religious dogma and old programming. To unlearn false teachings in order to embrace my true self and destiny.

In 2018, after coming to the conclusion that my mother was a malignant narcissist and my siblings were abusive, I made powerful changes in my life. During this timeline, I went full no contact with each of them. It was dark, lonely, and isolating. At the same time, it felt liberating, freeing, and cathartic. This is what my soul needed in effort to break free of toxic relationships.

My mother complicated the situation by persistently manipulating me, hovering me, and baiting me. She refused to respect my healthy boundaries. No matter how much I tried to distance myself from her, she'd suck me back into her drama.

My toxic siblings and their families had bullied me, gaslit me, stalked me, and re-traumatized me. Their psychologically abusive behaviors were beyond contempt. Their smear campaigns on social media were abhorrent. They played barbarous tricks using alias accounts and pretending to be someone who they were not. Of course, I saw right through their pathetic smokescreens.

This was the start of 'the dark night of the soul' for me. The dark night of the soul is a term that is typically used to describe a period of *spiritual transformation*. However, it can feel heavy, suffocating, unbearable, and include significant suffering.

It's when your soul is in a wrestling match with your ego. Simply stated, your ego must die for your soul to thrive. The dark night of the soul can teach you valuable lessons if you are open and willing to receive it. Resisting it can sabotage your soul growth.

From 2018 through the present time, I've been open to my spiritual awakening. It has been by far the most incredible, life-changing experience. My soul had a deep longing for me to heal. This led me onto a beautiful journey of a soul transformation. It drastically shifted my old beliefs, my perspectives, my mindset, and my entire life.

There were divine signs that guided me. I learned to trust myself and the amazing process. It was not coincidental that I began seeing supernatural signs everywhere. Awesome synchronicities, including red cardinals, hawks, mourning doves, butterflies, rainbows, vivid dreams, visions in a waking state, and recurring numbers, especially 111, 333, and 555.

Hidden Blessings in Disguise

Sometimes, along our spiritual journey we can experience hidden blessings in disguise. In March 2019, one morning I awoke with my dad on my mind. It was a heavy feeling, which I couldn't shake. Something deep within my spirit whispered, *"You need to call dad. Something is wrong."*

Through the years, from my teens to my adulthood, I've had an 'inner knowing.' It is when you know about a specific situation without having to be told. Nobody informed me about my father, nor his medical status. I didn't receive any updates or information from my siblings.

During this time, I had been no contact with my entire family of origin. Due to my dad's advanced Alzheimer's, his severe cognitive impairment, and my sisters who triangulated my relationship with my dad, I had stopped contact with him. Truly, it had nothing to do with my dad. More so, when you go no contact with one relative, you can end up no contact with other relatives, especially if there's ongoing manipulation.

The reality was that even if I had called my father, visited him out of state, or sent him cards, there was a strong chance he wouldn't know it's me. Or my siblings would interfere by stealing my cards or letters that I had sent to my dad and dispose of them without him knowing.

In June 2018, when I drove out of state to visit my father, he didn't recognize me or my husband. It wasn't until I gave my dad gifts when he realized who I was. As he unwrapped and admired a framed photograph of him and I, suddenly he had a moment of lucidity. Excitedly, he exclaimed, *"Dana! It's you! You are here. I'm tickled pink!"*

Instantly, my dad wrapped his arms around me to give me a warm hug. It was a memorable moment that's forever ingrained in my mind. This memory of my dad fills me with peace, especially after what transpired on the morning of March 13, 2019.

On that morning, intuition prompted me to contact the residential care facility where my dad lived. He had been transitioned into hospice care. Feeling unsettled by my inner knowing, I picked up the phone, dialed the number, and gave the receptionist my dad's name for who I wished to speak to. Nervously, she stuttered, *"Ummm...let me get the supervisor."*

Then she placed me on hold. My heart raced with uncertainty! I silently prayed, *"Please let my father be fine."*

When the supervisor greeted me on the phone, I inquired about my dad. In a detached tone of voice, she confided, *"Your father passed away on March 11, 2019."*

As tears poured down my face, I asked, *"Was he in physical pain? What are his funeral arrangements? Please give me information."*

Hesitating, the supervisor deflected, *"I don't know your father's funeral arrangements. When he passed away, he wasn't in physical pain. We sedated him with medications."*

She could deny that she was unaware of my dad's funeral arrangements, but I knew for a fact that nursing homes have on file specific funeral arrangements. Following this phone call, my husband contacted several residential care facilities to inquire about their protocols. Each facility confirmed they must have on file the patient's arrangements for death, funerals, and/or memorial arrangements.

I had no doubt that my sisters were behind this illicit scheme to prevent me from knowing facts pertaining to my dad being on his deathbed (they never informed me), my dad passing away (they intentionally withheld vital information), his memorial and/or funeral arrangements (not a single relative informed me), and withholding legal information about my dad, including me being his beneficiary in his trust fund (they didn't inform me for close to two years.)

My sisters repeatedly created discord between my father and I. They would sneak behind my back and purposely manipulate whatever they could control. They created smear campaigns against me on Facebook YouTube and Twitter. They spent years harassing me. They manipulated me, spied on my website, and social media accounts, oftentimes writing cruel remarks. They tried to destroy me, my reputation, and my writing career. And they call themselves 'good Christians.'

To add to my turmoil, my siblings abused whatever power they had, especially with my father's estate, his trust fund, and his medical care. This was another slap in the face to me. It was their way to punish me for speaking the truth about my psychologically abusive birth family.

Following the painful news of my dad passing away without my being informed, I deeply grieved. I cried a river. I mourned for what my siblings stole from me; the chance to say goodbye to my dad. I lamented for the father I never had; my mother and siblings spent a lifetime triangulating my relationship with him. I cried for my inner child who had spent five decades trying to heal painful father wounds. In the midst of my loss and grief, I felt relieved that I had visited my dad in June 2018.

On that visit, my father shared personal stories with me. To my surprise, I had never heard about them prior to this. He discussed how he loved writing poetry as a teenager, which I didn't know. He shared his war stories and the trauma he experienced in the military. He even talked about his own father wound and how his dad had a father wound.

On that meaningful visit with my dad, there were times when he'd forget who I was, and he didn't recognize me, nor did he recognize my husband. My father graciously said, *"I apologize, but I don't know who you are, but I appreciate you spending time with me."*

On the last day when my husband and I were saying goodbye to my dad, he reverted back to a childhood state. Filled with fear, he trembled, *"I'm scared. I don't know where my room is. What if I get lost? What if I cannot find my way back?"*

Calmly, I comforted him. I hugged him and assured him, *"You are safe. The staff who works here will help you find your room. Everything will be okay. I love you, dad. I'm going to miss you."*

For one final time, I embraced my father in my arms. Choked up, it was hard to talk. I couldn't stop the tears from falling. On that summer afternoon when I said goodbye to my dad, my inner knowing was certain that this was the last time to see him alive. My gut instinct strongly sensed it.

I spent a long drive home reflecting on gratitude. I was grateful to have the opportunity to spend such a special weekend him. I will treasure it forever. As peace washed over me, I chose to focus on the good. My dad loved me and I loved him. My father wound had fully healed. Nobody could steal this from me. Not even my toxic siblings who despised me.

Fast forward to June 2019, one month after my dad passed away. On a sunny afternoon, my husband and I were strolling on a path in the park. Unexpectedly, I noticed a small rainbow in the sky. It looked more like a prism with gorgeous shades of red, orange, green, blue, and yellow. What mystified me was that it wasn't raining. The weather was perfect.

Intrigued by the colorful prism, I snapped a few pictures of it. Later on, I shared the photographs on Twitter. Instantly, two of my friends sent me private messages. They both confirmed there was an angel next to the rainbow in the sky.

When I took a closer glimpse at my pictures, I could see an angel. My two friends said they believed this was my dad's soul in an angelic form. They believed he was watching over me. One of my friends who's an empath shared, *"I sense your father has sent you a message. He said that he loves you and he's proud of you."*

This incredible experience was touching and emotional for me. At once, tears slipped down my face. I considered it a beautiful blessing in disguise. I may not have been able to say a final goodbye to my father, but he blessed me by this divine angelic sign.

I felt the presence of a God upon me. An unconditional love and light surrounded me. It's hard to articulate a spiritual experience. Those of you who've also had angelic encounters or divine signs, you know what I'm talking about. It is super miraculous.

There is something so much bigger than us. We may not always visually see it with our eyes. Yet, energetically and on another dimensions, there's a Higher Power on a spiritual realm.

Angels are fascinating spiritual beings. They not only serve a role as special messengers, but they are also warriors on behalf of us to protect us. I have experienced many angelic encounters in my lifetime. *"See, I am sending an angel before you to protect you on your journey and to lead you safely to the place I have prepared for you."* (Exodus 23:20 NLT)

My spiritual awakening prompted me to listen to the soft voice within me. To trust myself and my gut instincts. To know my intuition will never lead me astray. A Higher Source has my best interests at heart.

Monarch Butterflies & Divine Signs

The most remarkable change that has taken place in my spiritual awakening is my perception about my narcissistic mother. My thoughts, perspective, and beliefs have radically shifted over the past three years. I view things in a whole new light.

Two days before my mother passed away, my nephew informed my son. Instantly, my son texted me of the news. It baffled me that not a single sister of mine had the decency to tell me that our mom was on her deathbed. Prior to this, I had no awareness about her being in hospice. As always, my siblings were intentionally trying to hurt me. Had it not been for my nephew sharing this important information with my son, I wouldn't have known.

Due to the Covid-19 pandemic, there was no way I could see my mom. According to my nephew, the hospice wouldn't permit her to have visitors, unless each one had undergone medical testing and clearances to prove they were not ill. No doubt, this could take many days, if not much longer.

My nephew told my son that my mom's organs in her body were shutting down. He expected her to pass away quickly. Obviously, I had no control over these circumstances.

I felt sad about how my mother's life would end. That our relationship hadn't been restored. Despite my mom deeply hurting me and betraying me, I will always love her. On that hot summer day, I silently prayed for my mom, her soul, and for an easy transition into her life after death. I asked God to forgive her and to have mercy on her.

In the early morning on July 8, 2020, the 'golden child' of my family was with my mother when she passed away. This actually filled me with peace. It was an answer to prayer. Of all the people who could be with my mom during her last breath on earth, this is the sister who I believe could offer our mom compassion, love, and empathy. For this, I'm grateful.

One week after my mom had died, I had a vivid dream about her. It felt very intense, vivid, and real. As if my deceased mother visited me in my sleep.

In my dream, I was in the back yard of the home where I had grown up with my birth family. My four older sisters were with me. They quietly stood near me. We were aware that our mother had passed away.

Suddenly, hundreds of Monarch butterflies surrounded me. They flew all around me and above me. In my dream, I knew my mother's spirit was with me. I could feel her soul near me. Visually I didn't see her physical body. Yet, I had no doubt she was present.

Within minutes, my mother's physical body appeared. She looked much younger and healthier. My mom moved closer to me, placed her arms around me, and gently hugged me. In my dream, I sensed that her soul made peace with my soul. It was on a spiritual realm and it felt telepathic.

As my mother and I embraced, I wept. It felt deeply moving and poignant. When I awoke from my dream, tears were still streaming down my cheeks.

Following my enlightening dream, it has helped me to view my situation with my narcissistic mother in a whole new light. To understand that she taught me valuable life lessons. Important teachable moments even if some of the lessons were painful and had wrecked me.

Valuable lessons to take back my positive energy and power. Life lessons to stand strong in my core self. To know that some people come into our lives to teach us difficult lessons and painful lessons. It is meant to wake us up to rescue our own soul.

I strongly believe that my soul desires me to be at peace with my mom. To release all resentment and negativity. To forgive her for abusing me and traumatizing me. This is freeing! I feel lighter, joyful, and liberated.

A core component of trauma recovery takes place on a spiritual level. It goes well beyond traditional counseling, talk therapy, or basic life coaching. Trauma pierces the soul. Narcissistic abuse is a form of soul murder. Therefore, our soul requires healing.

Due to the long-term consequences of narcissistic abuse, toxic relationships, sexual assaults, and child abuse, the missing piece of the puzzle is doing soul work. Traditional therapists and/or Certified Trauma Recovery Coaches need to be able to work with survivors on a spiritual level (not just physical, emotional, or relational) because narcissistic abuse and trauma are a form of soul defilement.

Trauma recovery requires you to reconnect yourself to your soul. Otherwise, you remain disconnected. I refer to this as '***soul rescue***.' For over a year, I've felt nudged to write a sixth book with this title. I've known this book is meant to take a deep dive into healing narcissistic abuse and trauma; physically, emotionally, but especially spiritually.

It's no coincidence that exactly one year ago on the day I received a spiritual download to write *Soul Rescue*, I received a confirmation to start writing this very book. As usual, I prayed for divine signs. I asked to specifically see mourning doves. SNAP! Just like that, mourning doves crossed my path. Not only once, but twice within 24 hours. Ever since then, I've been seeing mourning doves everywhere.

14 Signs You Are Spiritually Awakening:

1. You desire to know your purpose for being here on earth.
2. You start soul-searching, which involves a process of introspection.
3. You are more aware of toxic people & toxic energies around you.
4. You experience the dark night of the soul.
5. You crave for inner peace, solitude, & being in nature.
6. You feel deeper empathy & compassion towards others.
7. You have a shift in your perspectives & prior beliefs.
8. You experience heightened intuition & an inner knowing of certain things even though you were not officially informed about it.
9. You step into your authentic self & become a truth seeker.

10. You experience divine signs, synchronicities, visions, dreams, supernatural phenomena, intuitiveness, & major transformations.
11. You realize that all human beings are interconnected. You desire to help & serve others.
12. Instead of judging other people, you consider their cultural & religious beliefs & respect them for their differences.
13. You have a higher level of well-being & a more consistent mind-body connection.
14. You have a moment of realization that life is beyond all material things.

To accelerate your spiritual awakening, you can meditate, pray, journal and/or spend time in solitude. You can become more in tune with yourself and your energy. Start practicing gratitude, mindfulness, meditation, self-love, acceptance, and manifesting positivity into your life. During your spiritual journey, you can reconnect to nature, to your dreams, your pets, your inner child, your creativity, and spending time with likeminded empathic people who lift your spirits higher.

> *"We are all equally capable of spiritual awakening. It may not seem that way, at times. Some of us are so caught up in the drama of our day-to-day existence that we have lost track of who we really are. But eventually, all of us will make the discovery of our true nature."*
>
> Victor Shamas

FOURTEEN

The Devastating Toxic Family Legacy

"Perfectionistic parents see, to operate under the illusion that if they can just get their children to be perfect, they will be a perfect family. They put the burden of stability on the child to avoid facing the fact that they, as the parents, cannot provide it. The child fails and becomes the scapegoat for family problems. Once again, the child is saddled with the blame."

Dr. Susan Forward, author of *Toxic Parents: Overcoming Their Hurtful Legacy and Reclaiming Your Life*

Unhealthy, toxic families discourage their children to be unique. They frown upon their children to embrace their special strengths, personalities, and self-expression. Each child must conform to the rigid thoughts, behaviors, and belief system of the dysfunctional family unit.

The narcissistic parent promotes fusion, a blurring of personal boundaries, and an enmeshment of intergenerational trauma, which passes from one generation to the next. In their manipulation to pretend they have a 'perfect family,' they often suffocate one another's individuality.

I am devastated by my own toxic family legacy. I absolutely don't want this passed onto my children and future generations. It disturbs me about horrendous neglect and abuse, which began hundreds of years before I was born. My ancestry bloodline is riddled with generations of ongoing child abuse, sexual abuse, physical abuse, addictions, and mental abuse by one or more lethal parents.

In some cases, the parent was a malignant narcissist. In other cases, they were grown adults who never healed their trauma. Instead, they dumped their baggage onto their innocent children and/or spouse.

It pains me that I was unaware of this reality in my younger years. More so, it wrecks me that I didn't understand intergenerational trauma, especially as a young woman when I gave birth to my three beautiful children. As a mother, I don't want the intergenerational trauma to carry into the lives of my kids. This is why I am now making significant changes in my life with my adult children. For the wounds of our ancestry must be processed, understood, and released for each of us to heal.

In my early 40's when I was diagnosed with fibromyalgia, my Aunt Joan shared her own fibromyalgia journey with me. She discussed her past sexual abuse by her father, how she had chronic pain, and a diagnosis of fibromyalgia. My Aunt Joan and I became very close. We seemed to have many things in common.

Oftentimes, we emailed one another and I learned a lot about my dad's side of the family. It broke my heart that my Aunt Joan spent years suffering physical, emotional, and sexual abuse by the hands of her dad; my grandfather. As I read her letter, I cringed at how my intoxicated grandpa would return home from the bar, sneak into my Aunt Joan's bedroom, and molest her. Not just once or twice. Rather, for many years.

My Aunt Joan confided that fibromyalgia is a direct result of abuse. She encouraged me to read the book by Dr. John Sarno, *Healing Back*

Pain: The Body-Mind Connection. My Aunt Joan raved about his book, saying it healed her and she was free of fibromyalgia.

Inspired by my Aunt Joan's miraculous results, I ordered several books by Dr. John Sarno. In my personal experience, I didn't receive a healing after reading those books. However, I did come to learn much more about the body and mind connection to abuse.

In his hallmark book, *The Body Keeps the Score: Brain, Mind, and Body in the Healing of Trauma,* Bessel van der Kolk expresses physical and emotional experiences of children in the narcissistic family. He wrote, *"Trauma almost invariably involves not being seen, not being mirrored, and not being taken into account. Being able to feel safe with other people is probably the single most important aspect of mental health."*

Angie Atkinson, an author, narcissistic abuse expert, and YouTuber, sheds light on unhealthy mirroring in the toxic family. She states, *"Mirroring is the usually subconscious replication of another person's nonverbal signals. In layman's terms, mirroring is when you reflect back the mannerisms, behaviors, and other behaviors of other people. It causes us to adopt different facial expressions, body language, as well as tone. Worse, the lack of mirroring in infancy can lead to a very toxic legacy in your family. When a mother doesn't naturally mirror her babies, chances are she didn't receive mirroring in her own infancy and early childhood. As a result, unless she chooses to develop the awareness needed to overcome this and to intentionally change the pattern, she won't be able to offer it to her kids either. This leads to her trauma being passed on to her children, and this can continue in families for generations."*

What do toxic family members mirror to the scapegoat? They mirror this negative message:

- You are not good enough.
- You are the problem.
- You don't deserve love or kindness.
- You are not important.

- Your life has no value or worth.

Bonnie Badenoch, author of *The Heart of Trauma: Healing the Embodied Brain the Context of Relationships*, wrote, "*If people have harmed us, that part is usually a protector whose need to cause injury comes from desperate attempts to not feel destroyed by the pain and fear they are carrying. Generally, they are not conscious of this process, but it likely mirrors what has been passed down through the generations in the family.*"

What is a family legacy? How can it impact your health, self-esteem, and life? According to CollinsDictionary.com, legacy is defined as "*A gift by will, especially of money or personal property. Something handed down or received from an ancestor or predecessor.*"

Legacy is also known as your birthright, endowment, inheritance, and tradition. A toxic legacy is a destructive pattern of harmful, painful, and damaging behaviors, which have been handed down from one generation to another. It's when one or more parent's and/or relatives repeatedly interact in a family system in unhealthy ways. These dysfunctional family unit imprint their family members with psychologically damaging words and behaviors.

Intergenerational trauma significantly impacts the structure of each family. Instead of children growing up feeling secure, cared for, respected, and loved, they are raised in a poisonous environment feeling rejected, emotionally abandoned, criticized, and unloved.

10 Devastating Results of a Toxic Family Legacy:

1. **Lack of Trust** – From early on, children who are abused by a parent and/or other relatives, learn to not trust anyone, including their family. They learn their own mother, father, grandparents, and siblings are not safe. If their narcissistic parent bullied them, they start to question themselves. They may second-guess their own reality. Sometimes, they feel as if

they're going crazy. They lack trust in other people, which is a normal trauma response.

2. **Silence** – The lethal family system has a code of silence. The abused child will become withdrawn, quiet, and may be very shy. If they dare speak out and protest the unfairness of the abuse, they will oftentimes experience corporal punishment. Through time, they learn that silence may protect them as a child. However, as a grown adult, silence may not keep you safe. Silence may prevent you from seeking help. Silence steals your voice.
3. **Codependency** – A toxic home goes hand in hand with codependent relationships with your parents, siblings, relatives, and even future relationships with intimate partners. According to Merriam Webster.com, "*Codependency is a psychological condition or a relationship in which a person is controlled or manipulated by another who is affected with a pathological condition.*" Here's a quote that is spot on about codependent relationships. "*Codependence is an imbalanced relationship pattern where one partner assumes a high-cost 'giver-rescuer' role and the other is the 'taker-victim' role.*" ~ Shawn Meghan Burn, PhD., author of *Unhealthy Helping: A Psychological Guide for overcoming Codependence, Enabling, and Other Dysfunctional Helping*
4. **Toxic shame & blame-shifting** – The narcissistic parent and/or siblings dump all of the toxic shame and blame onto the family scapegoat. They accuse the scapegoat of being the perpetrator. They claim, "*It's your fault and you deserve to be mistreated.*"

Narcissistic parents violate boundaries, play family members against one another, continue the toxic family legacy, and abuse their power. Sadly, children in such toxic homes are treated to normalize day-to-day neglect and abuse, which is clouded by fear, denial, anxiety, and isolation.

Parents with the traits and/or diagnosis of narcissistic personality disorder (NPD) are pathologically hyper-focused on themselves. They're incapable of the unconditional love and acceptance children need for secure emotional attachment and growth. In the abusive family, the narcissist's needs trump all else. Children are manipulated to support those needs at great expense, often growing up to become adults with CPTSD or PTSD.

Dr. Brene Brown is the world's leading researcher on shame, vulnerability, courage, and empathy. One of her powerful quotes says, *"Shame, blame, disrespect, betrayal, and the withholding of affection damage the roots from which love grows. Love can only survive these injuries if they are acknowledged, and healed. If we can share our story with someone who responds with empathy and understanding, shame can't survive."*

5. **Perfectionism & Control** – Due to the narcissist being extremely controlling and abusing their power, it's common for their children to grow up feeling inadequate and powerless. In addition, in most cases, the abused children feel the need to be perfect in order to win the love, acceptance, and approval of the narcissist, toxic siblings, and other relationships.
6. **Adverse Childhood Experiences (ACEs)** – The most-deadly impact of the toxic family legacy is to cause severe long-term damage to children. According to the Center of Disease Control & Prevention, *"Adverse Childhood Experiences (ACEs) are potentially traumatic events that occur in childhood. ACEs can include violence, abuse, sexual assault, and growing up in a family with mental health or substance use problems."* Toxic stress from ACEs can change brain development and affect how the body responds to stress. ACEs are linked to chronic health problems, mental illness, CPTSD, addictions, and trauma.
7. **Betrayal Trauma** – When you're growing up, you expect to be supported, protected, loved, and taken good care of by your family. However, in a dysfunctional home, there is betrayal of an innocent child's trust of his/her parents, siblings, and

relatives. Physical abuse, mental abuse, sexual abuse, neglect, and invalidation scars the child with a deep sense of betrayal. Your core sense of who you are is destroyed. It undermines your self-confidence, self-esteem, and belief that the world is a loving, safe place. Therefore, your trust is shattered.

8. **Addictions** – Dr. Gabor Mate' who specializes in addictions and trauma believes there is a direct correlation between the two. When the trauma is repressed or suppressed, the person may unconsciously try to numb, detach, and dissociate from their abuse. They may not be aware of how their addictions are connected to their intense pain. Dr. Gabor Mate's intriguing quote shares, "*Not all addictions are rooted in abuse or trauma, but I do believe they can all be traced to painful experiences. A hurt is at the center of all addictive behaviors. It is present in the gambler, the Internet addict, the compulsive shopper, and the workaholic. The wound may not be as deep and the ache may not be as excruciating, and it may even be entirely hidden – but it's there.*"

9. **Deep Rooted Anger** – If you are the black sheep in your family or the scapegoat, you may experience anger. Based on your history of being abused, bullied, and manipulated, you may have what I refer to as 'righteous anger.' Considering everything you have suffered and endured, you have every right to feel your authentic human emotions, including anger. The National Center for PTSD confirms the link between anger and trauma. They said, "*Anger is often a large part of a survivor's response to trauma. It is a core piece of the survival response in human beings. Anger helps us cope with life's stresses by giving us energy to keep going in the face of trouble. Yet, anger can create major problems in the personal lives of those who have experienced trauma and those who suffer from PTSD.*"

10. **Family Estrangement** – It is no surprise that when you are raised in a dysfunctional family unit where there is ritual abuse, you can experience one or more broken relationships. Another name for going no contact is estrangement. A recent British survey defines family estrangement as "*The breakdown of*

> *supportive relationships between family members. The heartbreak of family estrangement is that those who are supposed to support you, don't. Those who should be on your side, aren't."* In the British study, over 50% of those estranged from a parent said that they cut off the contact. When asked why they went no contact with their parent, the estranged adult stated, *"We could never have a functional relationship again."*

Whether you have practiced the grey rock method or no contact rule with your toxic family, you may have dozens of logical reasons why you made this decision. In my experience with my own dysfunctional family, I went no contact with my narcissistic mother, siblings, and relatives due to the chronic bullying, gaslighting, manipulation, triangulation of relationships, and ongoing psychological abuse.

Dear Survivor, please understand that authentic love and abuse cannot co-exist. Love doesn't betray you. Love won't abandon you. Unconditional love will support you. Those who truly love you will accept your strengths and your flaws. They will love you as you are. And you will feel safe.

Author, Susan Forward, eloquently echoes the difference between love and abuse. She affirms, *"Most adult children of toxic parents grow up feeling tremendous confusion about what love means and how it's supposed to feel. Their parents did extremely unloving things to them in the name of love. They came to understand love as something chaotic, dramatic, confusing, and often painful—something they had to give up their own dreams and desires for. Obviously, that's not what love is all about. Loving behavior doesn't grind you down, keep you off balance, or create feelings of self-hatred. Love doesn't hurt, it feels good. Loving behavior nourishes your emotional well-being. When someone is being loving to you, you feel accepted, cared for, valued, and respected. Genuine love creates feelings of warmth, pleasure, safety, stability, and inner peace."*

Ending the cycle of intergenerational trauma was the key for me to start my healing journey. Self-preservation is necessary. It helped me give voice to my pain. In July 2018, I disclosed the truth on my YouTube channel about being a daughter of a narcissistic mother. After an outpouring of love, support, and thousands of comments from abuse survivors, I discovered that I was not alone.

If you grew up in a toxic family, have the courage to break your devastating legacy. Turn your pain into determination to end the dysfunctional patterns. Be the brave soul who breaks the abusive cycle of intergenerational trauma. Your new motto is: It stops here with me. Your children, grandchildren, and future generations deserve to be treated with tenderness, gentleness, kindness, and unconditional love.

Holistic Modalities to Support Your Trauma Recovery

For 12 years, I've been on an amazing healing journey. When I had a near death nightmare in November 2010, I looked outside the box for other ways to recover. I decided to be open to various holistic modalities to heal; physically, emotionally, mentally, and spiritually. It saved my life! For this I am eternally grateful.

While it started with trial and error, eventually I learned natural methods to reduce my fibromyalgia pain levels, to sleep better, to decrease anxiety, depression, and Complex PTSD symptoms, my back pain, and so much more. Along my healing journey, I learned that I have far more power to increase my health and quality of life than what Western Medicine claims. We each have the innate ability to heal. Gently. Gradually. Safely.

Using nature, bodywork, herbs, essential oils, a clean diet, and other methods, we can step into the driver seat to heal. One day at a time. Without toxic chemicals. Without invasive procedures. Without harming our body and mind with potentially destructive ingredients. Before we get into holistic modalities, let's first build awareness about various types of traumatic events.

Various Types of Traumas:

1. Sexual abuse
2. Child neglect & abuse
3. Physical abuse
4. Mental/Emotional abuse
5. Sibling Abuse
6. War-induced trauma
7. Natural disasters
8. Mass shootings
9. Bullying & harassment
10. Life-threatening illness
11. Medical Negligence/malpractice
12. Narcissistic Abuse
13. Domestic Violence

As mentioned before, trauma can cause people to disconnect. They disconnect from their own body, mind, soul, and present reality. Survivors may disconnect because the pain hurts badly. Most survivors are not aware that they have mentally, physically, and spiritually detached from themselves.

You cannot heal from a place of shame, denial, or detachment. You can't recover if you separate yourself from your mind, body, and soul. Healing your trauma requires you to reconnect to yourself. It is a beautiful experience to come home to your whole self.

Healing begins within. Listen to what your body is screaming for your attention. Your symptoms are alerting you. They're asking you to tend to your body sensations and emotions. This includes your body pain, inflammation, migraines, insomnia, anxiety, stomachaches, triggers, flashbacks, and triggers.

You may feel frozen in time. Stuck in your trauma. The goal is to not cover up your symptoms. Shift your focus. Observe them. Learn that each organ is connected to an underlying condition, which could be how your trauma has manifested itself into a physical or emotional illness.

Your trauma is not merely something from the past. You cannot forget it or just move on. Instead, trauma is within each cell in your body. There is a body-mind connection to trauma, including cellular memory and epigenetics.

In my recovery journey, my healing couldn't start until I was free from medicine. It was a fierce battle for my own life. My prescriptions masked the root cause of my trauma. Tapering each medicine was not an easy road to travel. It was by far the most traumatic, hellish ordeal for me, especially since several of my medications were severely interacting and causing me intense withdrawal symptoms.

While there is a time and place for medicine, it shouldn't be the first choice, nor only option. I've learned the hard way that prescriptions can numb the brain and our memory. It sabotaged my ability to process my pain. It prevented me to heal my trauma. I was traumatized by medical doctors who placed me in harms way and used poor judgement during my medical care.

It disturbs me that some traditional doctor's refuse to examine the root cause of the problem. They hand out one prescription after another. Then the patient may suffer negative side effects, serious implications, injuries, suicidal ideation and thoughts, worse depression and anxiety, and secondary trauma to their initial trauma.

Mind-warping psychotropic medications are not the solution. The drugs can alter the brain, memory, and cognitive function. It can suppress the patient's authentic emotions. It can take your life hostage in which you lose your control over your own mind, body, and life.

If there is nothing you learn today, I hope you can understand that we begin to heal only when we reconnect to ourselves to fully feel our emotions. We feel it to heal it. Even if it is uncomfortable. Even when it may not feel good. Even despite the dark moments when painful memories come into our conscious minds.

I love trauma expert, Dr. Bessel Van Der Kolk's quote, in which he states, "*Trauma is not an event that took place sometime in the past. It is also the imprint left by that experience on the mind, brain, and body.*" (The Body Keeps the Score book.)

Holistic Modalities for Healing Trauma:

1. EMDR, which stands for Eye Movement Desensitization and Reprocessing
2. Emotional Freedom Technique (EFT)
3. Professional massage therapy
4. Acupuncture
5. Energy healing
6. Myofascial release therapy
7. Music therapy
8. Art therapy
9. Pet therapy
10. Pure Essential oils
11. Herbalism
12. Homeopathy
13. Naturopathy
14. Trauma Sensitive Yoga
15. Meditation
16. Prayer
17. Cranial Sacral therapy
18. Breath work
19. Reiki Spiritual Healing
20. Bodywork
21. Sound therapy
22. Certified Trauma Recovery Coaching
23. Inner Child Work
24. Somatic Release therapy
25. Hypnotherapy
26. Spiritual Practices

27. Psychological Kinesiology
28. Journaling
29. Trauma Release Exercises (TRE)
30. Ayurveda

For additional professional resources for trauma recovery, please check the back of this book, *Soul Rescue,* which includes a wide variety of non-medical resources, books, holistic options, specialists, plus more.

There is no single pathway to trauma recovery. Instead, there are many different holistic modalities to pave the way from barely surviving to fully thriving. Similar to a garden, healing trauma requires removing the weeds in your life that keep you stuck. An old mindset. False beliefs. Toxic relationships. Physical and emotional pain that block you from fully healing.

You can weed out what no longer serves you. With nurturing, insight, education, and practical tools, you can embrace your true essence, which brings you back to wholeness. While I am not a therapist, nor do I give advice, I am more like a gentle guide, mentor, and teacher. In harmony, I walk beside you in a nonjudgmental way, as I offer you practical tools to process and heal your trauma.

Bloom from the Dark

I am an empowered author, speaker, educator, YouTuber, survivor, and Certified Trauma Recovery Coach. I have a big heart for survivors. I'm passionately advocating on their behalf. I provide professional trauma-informed safe space to heal on your own timeline. My clients have voice and choice in however they choose to heal.

A lotus flower is a metaphor for trauma recovery. The lotus flower symbolizes inner strength, purity, spiritual awakening, and wisdom. It takes courage and strength to keep growing from the darkness and emerge into the light.

The conditions that produce the lotus flower are dark and harsh, but it never gives up. Despite the fierce opposition and darkness, the lotus flower blooms most beautifully from the deepest mud. It is a positive reminder that just like the lotus flower, you can break free from your trauma wounds to wonderfully flourish.

As a Certified Trauma Recovery Coach, I work one on one with clients in private coaching sessions to help them gently unpack their trauma. It's therapeutic and empowering when you give voice to your inner child. It's like you are coming home to yourself; beautifully blossoming!

We don't need eloquent words to support trauma survivors. Our calm presence and willingness to hear someone's story can make a major difference. **When we bear witness to their pain, they no longer feel so alone.** Being heard, seen, and validated is therapeutic.

When we walk in the darkness beside trauma survivors, we can be a healing balm to help them find the light within them. May you bravely shine your beautiful light. If you need emotional support, feel free to reach out to me on my website to inquire about my coaching services.

Soul Rescue

"As traumatized children we always dreamed that someone would come and save us. We never dreamed that it would, in fact, be ourselves, as adults."

Alice Little

Dear Courageous Survivor, you have endured hardships. You have been heartbroken. You have overcome fierce trials. You may have felt lost and betrayed. Yet, look how far you have come. You are still standing! You are transforming as a human being. You are moving forward.

I am so proud of you. Despite how painful or stressful your healing journey has been, you are doing the hard work to recover. You have stood up for yourself in the face of intense opposition.

You are worthy of being seen, heard, believed, respected, validated, supported, and loved. No matter how relentless your battles are, you have fought the good fight. In the midst of your brutal struggles, you have found the strength to rescue your own self.

YOU DID IT! I am honored to be a part of your trauma recovery. Best wishes to you in your healing journey.

THANK YOU!

Dear Readers and Trauma Survivors, thank you for taking the time to read *Soul Rescue: How to Break Free from Narcissistic Abuse & Heal Trauma.* For those who found my book therapeutic, empowering, or helpful along your own healing journey, I would be honored if you would write a review on Amazon and/or Goodreads. Truly, there is no greater gift to an author than supportive readers who post honest reviews to share books that have helped them or inspired them.

My Amazon author profile:
https://www.amazon.com/Dana-Arcuri/e/B00HF97MVO/ref=sr_ntt_srch_lnk_1?qid=1546967863&sr=8-1

My Goodreads author profile:
https://www.goodreads.com/author/show/6451514.Dana_Arcuri

Best Wishes to Your Healing Journey,

Dana

Acknowledgments

To my husband, Tony: Mere words cannot express how much I care about you and how blessed I am to share the past thirty-four years with you. From the bottom of my heart, thank you for always being dedicated to me and for being my rock to depend on. Lastly, thank you for understanding my trauma, for supporting me, for believing in me, and for walking next to me along my healing journey. I love you to the moon and back!

To my children: Each of you are a beautiful blessing who gives me so much joy. My life would not be complete without each of you being part of it. During the past few years, the three of you have played a vital role in my awakening to the dysfunction in my birth family. Thank you so much for encouraging me to create healthier boundaries and for supporting me in the decisions that I have made. I pray for the three of you to embrace your wonderful talents, strengths, and to pursue your deepest aspirations. I am proud of each of you and love you so much.

To Beth Jones: Ten years ago, when I didn't believe in myself, my writing ability, or my purpose, you planted positive seeds within me. You have been a big part of my stepping out of my comfort zone to follow my writing, speaking, and coaching passions. Thank you for always believing in me, for encouraging me, and for cheering me on to follow my dreams.

To Trisha Fuentes: It was such a godsend to be referred to you by another author. Thank you so much for doing an excellent job at designing my front book cover, spine, and back cover for *Soul Rescue*. I absolutely love it! In addition, I am grateful for your professional formatting and expertise. Much appreciation for your artistic talent and support.

To my YouTube & Twitter Followers: Thank you for your ongoing support, encouragement, and kindness. I appreciate each one of you and your positive comments. Had it not been for the #MeToo movement in 2017, I don't know that I would have broken the silence about my child abuse, narcissistic abuse, and sexual assaults. Thank you for helping me to realize that I wasn't alone and giving me the courage to speak up. Together, in solidarity, we are making a significant difference to build awareness, to educate, to advocate, and to empower the world around us.

About the Author

Dana Arcuri is a captivating author, speaker, trauma-informed advocate, survivor, and a Certified Trauma Recovery Coach. She is a graduate of the International Association of Trauma Recovery Coaching. Dana empowers women and men to transform their lives. She passionately offers empathy, education, and holistic healing to our world; one survivor at a time.

She's the author of *Soul Cry: Releasing & Healing the Wounds of Trauma, Sacred Wandering: Growing Your Faith in the Dark, Reinventing You; Simple Steps to Transform Your Body, Mind, & Spirit, Harvest of Hope Devotional,* the memoir, *Harvest of Hope, Living Victoriously Through Adversity,* and a contributing author for *Inspired Women Succeed.*

As a freelance writer, her work has been published in *Christian Women Lifestyle xPress Online Magazine, Pearls of Promise Ministries, Write Where It Hurts, Seriously Write,* and Oprah Winfrey and Deepak Chopra's *21 days Manifesting Grace Through Gratitude.* In 2018, Dana was a featured speaker for the *Women's Power Surge Conference.*

She's been a speaker for the radio shows, *Wove Ministries, Beauty from the Ashes, Moving Forward in Faith,* and *Your Journey to Freedom.* In 2015, she had the honor of being nominated as one of 100 Top Faith Blogs for Christian Women on *Women's Bible Cafe.*

When Dana's not busy writing, she enjoys dark chocolate, reading, and bird watching. You may visit her at the following websites:

Dana's website:
https://danaarcuri.com

Amazon:
https://www.amazon.com/Dana-Arcuri/e/B00HF97MVO

Twitter:
Dana Arcuri (@DanaLArcuri) / Twitter

YouTube:
https://www.youtube.com/channel/UCtpAeg5l19dcDuDPyKs6kJw?view_as=subscriber

Goodreads:
https://www.goodreads.com/author/show/6451514.Dana_Arcuri

Professional Resources for Survivors

Are you struggling with Complex PTSD, anxiety, flashbacks, triggers, or chronic pain? Perhaps, you are a trauma survivor who's looking for practical ways to cope? Or you want to move beyond merely surviving to fully thriving?

If so, you've come to the right place. As a trauma survivor, author, speaker, trauma-informed advocate, and Certified Trauma Recovery Coach, I know what it's like to feel stuck in old patterns. I understand the normal trauma response of being slammed with fight, flight, freeze, or fawn mode. Or unexpectedly being triggered and having flashbacks.

We don't want to be repeatedly going around and around in a vicious cycle. This is why I have created a professional list of trauma resources. Because sometimes asking for help or obtaining emotional support is the first step to our trauma recovery.

If you are currently in the midst of picking up the shattered pieces of your past abuse, please know that: I hear you. I see you. I believe you. Your life and health matter. You deserve to heal.

Remember that the diamond didn't become a radiant, beautiful diamond easily. Instead, it had to first be refined through the fire. Like a sparkling diamond, you are being refined. May you have the courage and strength to shine brightly.

> *"A diamond doesn't start out polished and shining. It once was nothing special, but with enough pressure and time, becomes spectacular."*
>
> Solange Nicole

Adult Survivors of Child Abuse

Emma-Jane Taylor, Author| Speaker| Activist focused on Child Sex Abuse - Emma-Jane is a globally recognized voice on the subject of Child Sex Abuse. As a survivor she understands the importance of listening and sharing nonjudgmental support for the many Child Sex Abuse survivors around the world suffering in silence. She has given comment to the Bill Cosby case in Grazia magazine, the UKs National Press and was the Keynote Speaker for the NSPCC's largest fundraising event in the UK, 2021. For details on her work or to share your voice on her platform – her door is always open to you. www.emmajanetaylor.com

National Association of Adult Survivors of Child Abuse – The founder is Bill Murray who is also a recovering adult survivor of severe abuse and he's the CEO of NAASCA since 9/11/01. NAASCA is an all-volunteer group who works to educate, inform, and prevent all forms of child abuse and trauma – physical abuse, psychological trauma, sexual assault, verbal abuse, and neglect. They support anyone from all walks of life with their recovery. They educate the public about the pandemic of child abuse, teaching what can be done to prevent it. All the services and information they offer is free. https://www.naasca.org

Adult Trauma Survivors of Alcoholics & Dysfunctional Families

Adult Survivors of Alcoholics & Dysfunctional Families (ACA) – They are a Twelve Step, Twelve Tradition program of people who grew up in dysfunctional homes. They meet to share their experiences of growing up in an environment where abuse, neglect, and trauma infected them. They believe this affects them today and influences how they deal with all aspects of their lives. ACA provides a safe, nonjudgmental environment that allows survivors to grieve their childhoods and conduct an honest inventory of themselves and their families – so they may identify and heal core trauma, experience freedom from shame and abandonment, and become their own loving parents. https://www.adultchildren.org

Adverse Childhood Experiences (ACE)

Center for Disease Control & prevention – Adverse Childhood Experiences (ACE) are potentially traumatic events that occur in childhood (0-17 years) such as experiencing violence, abuse, or neglect; witnessing violence in the home; and having a family member attempt or die by suicide. Also included are aspects of the child's environment that can undermine their sense of safety, stability, and bonding such as growing up in a household with substance misuse, mental health problems, or instability due to parental separation or incarceration of a parent, sibling, or other member of the household.

https://www.cdc.gov/violenceprevention/childabuseandneglect/acestudy/aboutace.html

Benzodiazepine & Mental Health

Benzodiazepine Information Coalition – They are a group of patients and medical professionals who believe the over-prescription of benzodiazepines without proper warning has resulted in a growing national epidemic of benzodiazepine injury. They seek to break the stigma and raise awareness around prescribed benzodiazepine injury, providing a voice to the patients who are suffering, and facilitate research and access to competent, evidence-based medical care for those impacted by benzodiazepine induced disability. https://www.benzoinfo.com/

Benzodiazepine Support Group – An online forum to connect with others experiencing similar challenges with benzodiazepines. http://www.benzobuddies.org/

Professor C Heather Ashton, DM, FRCP, Emeritus Professor of Clinical Psychopharmacology – Dr. Ashton had operated a benzodiazepine withdrawal clinic for 12 years, was the UK's leading expert for benzodiazepines. She is the author of *Benzodiazepines: How They Work and How to Withdraw*. The Ashton Manual, including its 2011 update provides a wealth of educational information pertaining to benzodiazepines, tapers, symptoms, withdrawals, and recovery. https://www.benzo.org.uk/manual/index.htm

Dr. Peter Breggin, M.D. – A psychiatrist, author, and speaker who advocates to reform the mental health field. He's the author of mental health books, including *Psychiatric Drug Withdrawal: A Guide for Prescribers, Therapists, Patients, and their Families*, published in 2013 and *Medication Madness: The Role of Psychiatric Drugs in Cases of Violence, Suicide, and Murder*, published in 2008. https://breggin.com/

Mad in America – A website designed to serve as a resource and community for those interested in rethinking psychiatric care in the United States and abroad. The purpose is to provide readers with news, recovery stories, access to source documents, and informed writings of bloggers. https://www.madinamerica.com/

Books on Boundaries

Boundaries: Where You End and I Begin – How to Recognize and Set Healthy Boundaries by Anne

Katherine Boundaries: Where You End and I Begin - How to Recognize and Set Healthy Boundaries: Anne Katherine: 9781568380308: Amazon.com: Books

Set Boundaries, Find Peace: A Guide to Reclaiming Yourself by Nedra Glover Tawwab -

Amazon.com: Set Boundaries, Find Peace: A Guide to Reclaiming Yourself: 9780593192092: Tawwab, Nedra Glover: Books

Powerful Boundaries: Own Your Energy & Ditch Toxic Relationships by Holly Tarry -

Power Boundaries: Own Your Energy & Ditch Toxic Relationships: Tarry, Holly: 9781951692087: Amazon.com: Books

Bullying, Harassment, & Stalking

Anti-Bullying Network – The Anti-Bullying Network was established at the University of Edinburgh in 1999 with funding from the Scottish Executive to provide free anti-bullying support to school communities. In the first eight years that it operated on this basis, the Network gained a national reputation for the high quality of the services it provided to school communities. The Anti-Bullying Network is now an independent operation with the following objectives:

- to support anti-bullying work in schools;
- to provide a free website;
- and to offer an anti-bullying service which will include the provision of training, publications and consultancy services.

info@antibullying.net and https://www.antibullying.net

NAPAB, Advocating for Children's Rights - We advocate on behalf of bullied children and their families. We help schools across the country begin their own Cool 2 Be Kind Chapters. We also provide education and support to parents, educators, children and the community at large in order to promote a harassment free society. 1-800-273-TALK https://www.napab.org/leadership

Stop Bullying Foundation – They are dedicated to raising awareness about bullying and looking for ways to stop bullying through education and art. Their intention is to bring an anti-bullying program into schools to change the bullying dynamics that goes on in communities everywhere. https://www.stopbullyingfoundation.org

The Stalking Prevention, Awareness, & Resource Center (SPARC) – They are a federally funded project providing education and resources about the crime of stalking. SPARC aims to enhance the response to stalking by education the professionals tasked with keeping stalking victims safe and holding offenders accountable. SPARC ensures that allied professionals have the specialized knowledge to identify and respond to the crime of stalking. https://www.stalkingawarness.org

Protection Against Stalking – They believe that every victim of stalking should have the support and protection they need, including access to a locally based specialist stalking advocate service. They understand the harmful effects of stalking on peoples' lives. They are committed to raise awareness of the signs and educating about the benefits of early prevention, while supporting victims of stalking in all communities across the UK.

https://www.protectionagainststalking.org

Certified Trauma Recovery Coaching

Bloom from the Dark: Certified Trauma Recovery Coaching – Dana Arcuri is a trauma-informed advocate, Certified Trauma Recovery Coach, trauma survivor, inspirational author, and speaker who offers survivors safe space to process, acknowledge, and unpack their trauma. In addition, she is a graduate of International Association of Trauma Recovery Coaching (IAOTRC). She specializes in child abuse, sexual assault, narcissistic abuse, dysfunctional families, Complex PTSD/PTSD, chronic pain, holistic modalities, intergenerational trauma, mental abuse, physical abuse, and spiritual abuse. For over ten years, Dana's been an empowering YouTube Creator who builds awareness and advocates about "hard to discuss topics," including narcissistic parents, toxic siblings, how to set clear boundaries, trauma recovery, and holistic health. https://www.danaarcuri.com

International Association of Trauma Recovery Coaching – In the Fall of 2017, the association was founded by Bobbi L. Parish, MA, CTRC-S. As a survivor of childhood abuse, Bobbi has used her graduate degree in Marriage and Family Therapy to work with other trauma survivors. In January 2014, she transitioned from providing therapy to providing coaching, pioneering a profession that had only begun. After experiencing how powerfully coaching helped trauma survivors heal, Bobbi decided to help others become Certified Trauma Recovery Coaches. As one person could help a limited number of survivors heal. Yet, teaching other coaches and sending them into the world would provide thousands of survivors with high quality, easily accessible help. To learn more about Bobbie, IAOTRC, certification, and their coaching directory, check each website.

https://traumarecoverycoaching.com/about

https://certifiedtraumarecoverycoaching.com/the-path-to-certification

https://certifiedtraumarecoverycoaching.com/directory-of-coaches

Children's Advocacy

Child Help National Child Abuse Hotline – They are dedicated to the prevention of child abuse. Serving the U.S. and Canada, the hotline is staffed 24 hours a day, seven days a week with professional crisis counselors – who through interpreters – provide assistance in over 170 languages. The hotline offers crisis intervention, information, and referrals to thousands of emergency social services and support resources. Hotline: 1-800-422-4453

https://www.childhelp.org/hotline/

National Center for Missing & Exploited Children – They are a private, nonprofit corporation whose mission is to help find missing children, reduce child sexual exploitation, and prevent child victimization. Hotline: 1-800-843-5678

http://api.missingkids.org/home

National Children's Advocacy Center (NCAC) – They are located in Huntsville, Alabama and they have revolutionized the United States' response to child sexual abuse. Since its creation in 1985, the NCAC has served as a model for the 1000+ Children's Advocacy Centers (CACs) now operating in the United States and in more than 34 countries throughout the world. Hotline:

1-800-422-4453 https://www.nationalcac.org/

Complex PTSD/PTSD

CPTSD FOUNDATION - Successfully equipping trauma survivors and practitioners with compassionate support, skills, and trauma-informed education since 2014. Toll-free in the US: 844-552-7873. International: 917-780-4750 CPTSD Foundation

Dr. Deb Lindh, ED.D - Dr. Deb is a PTSD Survivor-Warrior, Amazon Best Selling Author, Award-Winning Scholar Practitioner, and founder of the global Twitter Chat #PTSDandBeyond and the podcast PTSD and Beyond which were both launched to provide advocacy, support, and resources as well as hope, inspiration, education, and empowerment to everyone affected by and with Post-Traumatic Stress Disorder (PTSD). Dr. Deb's contributions to Post-Traumatic Stress Recovery stems from sharing her story, experiences, and medication-free recovery with surviving narcissistic child abuse.

https://mindfuleffect.com/

https://ptsdandbeyond.org

Cymbalta

Drug Secrets: What the FDA isn't telling – Insightful article about the dangers of Cymbalta.

https://slate.com/technology/2005/09/what-the-fda-isn-t-telling.html

Soul Cry: Releasing & Healing the Wounds of Trauma – Author, speaker, survivor, and Certified Trauma Recovery Coach, Dana Arcuri, shared her captivating true story of the horrifying outcome from taking Cymbalta as prescribed by her doctor. Following her diagnosis of fibromyalgia and taking Cymbalta, she was slammed with worse depression, suicidal thoughts, and a near death nightmare. Her gripping memoir gives insight into the potential dangers and risks of taking Cymbalta (Duloxetine.) Hanging onto a thread of hope, Dana walks you through her battle as she overcame her darkest moments. She tells the story of her toll of compounded trauma, including Fibromyalgia, wicked drug withdrawals, a near death nightmare, and Complex PTSD. Bravely, Dana tells her real, raw story. For anyone battling deep wounds, she hears your soul cry. She gives a powerful voice to the voiceless and hope to the hopeless. She empowers you to courageously release and heal your trauma. http://www.danaarcuri.com/

Soul Cry Book: Soul Cry: Releasing & Healing the Wounds of Trauma - Kindle edition by Arcuri, Dana. Health, Fitness & Dieting Kindle eBooks @ Amazon.com.

Cymbalta Lawsuits – Patients who were injured by Cymbalta have filed a lawsuit against the pharmaceutical company, Eli Lilly. https://www.drugwatch.com/cymbalta/lawsuits/

Domestic Violence

National Center on Domestic Violence, Trauma, & Mental Health – Their mission is to develop and promote accessible, culturally relevant, and trauma-informed responses to domestic violence and other lifetime trauma so that survivors and their children can access the resources that are essential to their safety and well-being. They provide training, support, and consultation to advocates, mental health and substance abuse providers, legal professionals, and policymakers as they work to improve agency and systems-level responses to survivors and their children. Their work is survivor defined and rooted in principles of social justice.

http://www.nationalcenterdvtraumamh.org/about/

National Domestic Violence Hotline – The National Violence Hotline is a nonprofit organization established in 1966 as a component of the Violence Against Women Act (VAWA). They provide lifesaving tools and immediate support to enable victims to find safety and live free from abuse. Hotline: 1-800-799-7233, https://www.thehotline.org/

Fibromyalgia

Jacob Teitelbaum, M.D. – A board certified internist and nationally known expert in the fields of chronic fatigue syndrome, fibromyalgia, sleep, and pain. Best-selling author of *From Fatigued to Fantastic*, published in October 2017 and *The Fatigue and Fibromyalgia Solution*, published in August 2013. https://secure.endfatigue.com/

Holistic Modalities for Trauma Recovery

Emotional Freedom Technique (EFT) - Evidence-based tapping is one of the healing methods used for trauma, including for PTSD. According to Evidence-based EFT Training, *"EFT is an evidence-based stress-relief technique that has been proven to effectively help with traumatic experiences. As a brain-based somatic release technique it tackles stress, fear, and trauma where it is produced – in the brain. Stress also gets locked into the body, so being a somatic-approach it releases the stress from the body too."* https://evidencebasedeft.com

Eye Movement Desensitization and Reprocessing (EMDR) – Trauma Recovery, EMDR Humanitarian Assistance Programs is increasing the use of Eye Movement Desensitization and Reprocessing (EMDR) therapies to treat trauma victims worldwide by expanding access to EMDR trained professionals. As stated on the website EMDR Humanitarian Assistance Programs, *"Francine Shapiro, PhD, an American psychologist, developed Eye Movement Desensitization and Reprocessing (EMDR) Therapy as a breakthrough therapy with special capacity to overcome the devastating effects of psychological trauma in the late 1980's. An ever-growing community of therapist soon saw directly its power to transform lives. At the same time, controlled research studies consistently demonstrated its efficacy and effectiveness. During this procedure, patients tend to "process" the memory in a way that leads to a peaceful resolution. This often results in increased insight regarding both previously disturbing events and long held negative thoughts about the self."* https://emdrhap.org

Somatic Experiencing International – Trauma is a fact of life. It does not, however, have to be a life sentence. That is a guiding principle of Somatic Experiencing® International (SEI). We exist to bring *education and training* to those who can help heal people with trauma, *hope* to those living with trauma, and *awareness* of trauma to related professional communities and the general public. SEI is dedicated to comprehensive public awareness of Somatic Experiencing® and how it can help heal trauma. We "help the helpers" —those directly involved with people experiencing trauma—by training them in the practice of Somatic Experiencing (SE™). https://traumahealing.org

Healing Father Wounds

John Finch – He is an author, speaker, filmmaker, and Life Coach for men. John Finch always struggled after his father committed suicide when he was eleven, but it wasn't until he was raising his own three daughters that he truly understood their futures relied on his coming to terms with his difficult past. To move forward, he needed to forgive both his father for choosing to leave, and himself for not being the best father he could be. This journey led to *The Father Effect*, a book containing practical help for anyone, man or woman, with a deep father wound from losing a dad through divorce, death, or disinterest. Through positive lessons on forgiveness and approachable advice on how to change your legacy as a parent, partner, and person, *The Father Effect* is the ultimate healing tool for anyone who has suffered the absence of a dad. https://www.thefathereffect.com

The Father Effect book: The Father Effect: Hope and Healing from a Dad's Absence: Finch, John, Atwood, Blake, Meeker MD, Meg: 9781478976868: Amazon.com: Books

Mind-Body Connection & Trauma

Dr. Arielle Schwartz – She is a clinical psychologist, author, consultant, and therapist trainer. She has a private practice in Boulder, Colorado providing psychotherapy, supervision, and consultation in Resilience Informed Therapy, which applies research on trauma recovery, EMDR therapy, and Somatic Psychology to form a strength-based, trauma treatment model. In addition, she's the author of the book, *The Post-Traumatic Growth Guidebook: Practical Mind-Body Tools to Heal Trauma, Foster Resilience, and Awaken Your Potential.*

Welcome | Dr. Arielle Schwartz (drarielleschwartz.com)

The Post-Traumatic Growth Guidebook: Practical Mind-Body Tools to Heal Trauma, Foster Resilience and Awaken Your Potential: Schwartz, Arielle: 9781683732679: Amazon.com: Books

Dr. Bessel van der Kolk, M.D. – He is the founder and medical director of the Trauma Center in Brookline, Massachusetts. He is also a professor of psychiatry at Boston University School of Medicine and director of the National Complex Trauma Treatment Network. In addition, he's the #1 New York Times best-selling author of the book, *The Body Keeps The Score: Brain, Mind, and Body in the Healing of Trauma.* In his book, he uses recent scientific advances to show how trauma literally reshapes both the body and brain, compromising the sufferers' capacities for pleasure, engagement, self-control, and trust. He explores innovative treatments – from neurofeedback and meditation to sports, drama, and yoga – that offer new paths to recovery by activating the brain's natural neuroplasticity. https://besselvanderkolk.net/index.html

Dr. Gabor Mate' – He is a renowned speaker and best-selling author who is highly sought after for his expertise on a range of topics, including child development, addiction, stress, chronic pain, and trauma. Dr. Mate' is the author of *When the Body Says No: The Cost of*

Hidden Stress, which explores the mind-body connection of medical conditions linked to stress.

https://drgabormate.com/

Dr. John Sarno, M.D. – He was a professor of Clinical Rehabilitation Medicine, New York University School of Medicine, and attending physician at the Howard A. Rusk Institute of Rehabilitation Medicine. From 1984 to 2006, Dr. Sarno wrote four books pertaining to pain disorders that he called Tension Myoneural Syndrome (TMS). Dr. Sarno is the New York Times best-selling author of *Healing Back Pain: The Mind-Body Connection.* https://johnesarnomd.com/

Peter A. Levine, PhD. – He is the originator and developer of *Somatic Experiencing* and the Director of The Somatic Experiencing Trauma Institute. Peter holds a doctorate degree in Medical Biophysics and Psychology. During his thirty-five-year study of stress and trauma, he has contributed to a variety of scientific and popular publications. Also, he's the best-selling author of the book, *Waking the Tiger: Healing Trauma* and the book *In an Unspoken Voice: How the Body Releases Trauma and Restores Goodness.* His book, *Unspoken Voice,* is based on the idea that trauma is neither a disease nor a disorder, but rather an injury caused by fright, helplessness and loss that can be healed by engaging our innate capacity to self-regulate high states of arousal and intense emotions. Enriched with a coherent theoretical framework and compelling case examples, the book elegantly blends the latest findings in biology, neuroscience and body-oriented psychotherapy to show that when we bring together animal instinct and reason, we can become more whole human beings. https://traumahealing.org/

Narcissistic Abuse Books

Will I Ever Be Good Enough?: Healing the Daughters of Narcissistic Mothers by Dr. Karyl McBride – Will I Ever Be Good

Enough?: Healing the Daughters of Narcissistic Mothers: McBride, Dr. Karyl: 9781439129432: Amazon.com: Books

You're Not Crazy – It's Your Mother: Understanding and Healing for Daughters of Narcissistic Mothers by Danu Morrigan -

You're Not Crazy - It's Your Mother: Understanding and Healing for Daughters of Narcissistic Mothers (Daughters of Narcissistic Mothers, 1): Morrigan, Danu: 9781506462158: Amazon.com: Books

Narcissistic Fathers: How to Deal With a Toxic Father and Complex PTSD by Caroline Foster - Narcissistic Fathers: How to Deal With a Toxic Father and Complex PTSD (Adult Children of Narcissists Recovery Books): Foster, Caroline: 9798612500094: Amazon.com: Books

Out of the Fog: Moving from Confusion to Clarity After Narcissistic Abuse by Dana Morningstar - Amazon.com: Out of the Fog: Moving from Confusion to Clarity After Narcissistic Abuse (Audible Audio Edition): Dana Morningstar, Dana Morningstar, Morningstar Media: Audible Books & Originals

How to Kill a Narcissist: Debunking the Myth of Narcissism and Recovering From Narcissistic Abuse by J.H. Simon -

How To Kill A Narcissist: Debunking The Myth Of Narcissism And Recovering From Narcissistic Abuse (1): Simon, J.H.: 9780648012801: Amazon.com: Books

Healing From Hidden Abuse: A Journey Through the Stages of Recovery from Psychological Abuse by Shannon Thoman, LCSW -

Amazon.com: Healing from Hidden Abuse: A Journey Through the Stages of Recovery from Psychological Abuse (Audible Audio Edition): Shannon Thomas LCSW, Wendy Tremont King, Tantor Audio: Audible Books & Originals

Psychopath Free: Recovering from Emotionally Abusive Relationships With Narcissists, Sociopaths, and Other Toxic People by Jackson MacKenzie -

Amazon.com: Psychopath Free (Expanded Edition): Recovering from Emotionally Abusive Relationships With Narcissists, Sociopaths, and Other Toxic People: 9780425279991: MacKenzie, Jackson: Books

Adult Children of Emotionally Immature Parents: How to Heal from Distant, Rejecting, or Self-Involved Parents by Lindsay C. Gibson -

Adult Children of Emotionally Immature Parents: How to Heal from Distant, Rejecting, or Self-Involved Parents: Gibson , Lindsay C.: 9781626251700: Amazon.com: Books

Healing Adult Children of Narcissists: Essays on The Invisible War Zone and Exercises for Recovery by Shahida Arabi - Amazon.com: Healing the Adult Children of Narcissists: Essays on The Invisible War Zone and Exercises for Recovery: 9780578480060: Arabi, Shahida: Books

Becoming the Narcissist's Nightmare: How to Devalue and Discard the Narcissist While Supplying Yourself by Shahida Arabi -

Amazon.com: Becoming the Narcissist's Nightmare: How to Devalue and Discard the Narcissist While Supplying Yourself (Audible Audio Edition): Shahida Arabi, Julie McKay, Audible Studios: Audible Books & Originals

Parental Alienation

Parental Alienation Awareness Organization USA – They were founded to provide support for anyone experiencing this family bond obstruction. We are a social network of chapters across America and we come together in physical meetings and Facebook groups to provide each other with various types of help and share relevant information and coping strategies to feel more empowered and for a sense of community. https://www.paaousa.org

Parental Alienation Anonymous (PA-A) – They are a fellowship that offers a program of recovery for the families and friends of ALIENATORS whether or not the alienator recognizes the existence of a problem or seeks help. Members give and receive comfort and understanding through a mutual exchange of experience, strength, and hope. Sharing of similar problems binds individuals and groups together in a bond that is protected by a tradition of anonymity.

https://www.parentalalienationannonymous.com

Sexual Assault Hotline

RAINN (Rape, Abuse, & Incest National Network) – They are the nation's largest anti-sexual violence organization. RAINN created and operates the National Sex Assault Hotline in partnership with more than 1,000 local sexual assault service providers across the country and operates the DoD Safe Helpline for the Department of Defense. RAINN also carries out programs to prevent sexual violence, help survivors, and ensure that predators are brought to justice. Hotline: 1-800-656-4673 https://www.rainn.org/

Assaulted Women's Helpline – This Canadian organization offers a 24-hour telephone and a TTY crisis line to all women who have experienced abuse. They provide counseling, emotional support, information, and referrals. The helpline is dedicated to working towards equality for all women. Hotline: 1-866-863-0511 http://www.awhl.org/

Male Survivors of Sexual Assault & Abuse

Male Survivor - Every man who has experienced sexual assault or abuse deserves access to a judgment-free space where he can heal on his own terms and without shame. For 25 years, the website MaleSurvivor has fostered a healing community where tens of thousands of men from more than 200 countries come together to find support, information, and most importantly, hope. Contact them at MaleSurvivor, P.O. Box 276, Long Valley, New Jersey 07853 https://malesurvivor.org

Suicide Prevention

American Foundation for Suicide Prevention – 1-800- 273- 8255 http://www.afsp.org/

Canadian Association for Suicide Prevention (CASP) - http://www.suicideprevention.ca/

International World-Wide Suicide & Crisis Hotlines -

http://www.suicidehotlines.com/international.html

National Suicide Hotlines USA – 1-800-784-2433, Deaf hotline: 1-800-799-4889

http://www.suicidehotlines.com/

Trauma Professionals

American Trauma Society – American Trauma Society (ATS) is dedicated to the elimination of needless death and disability from injury. Over the past 50 years, ATS has served as an advocate for the trauma care system, trauma prevention programs, and the victims of trauma and their families throughout the United States. Our goals are to prevent injury whenever possible, and to ensure optimal treatment when it does occur. http://www.amtrauma.org

Bloom from the Dark Certified Trauma Recovery Coaching – Dana Arcuri is a Certified Trauma Recovery Coach, graduate from the International Association of Trauma Recovery Coaching (IAOTRC), an inspiring author, speaker, YouTuber with over 8K subscribers, trauma-informed advocate, and a trauma survivor. She works with all walks of life in one-on-one private coaching sessions to help clients gently process and unpack their trauma. It's therapeutic and empowering when you give voice to your inner child. It's like you're coming home to yourself to beautifully blossom. http://www.danaarcuri.com

Made in United States
Orlando, FL
23 November 2021